UC Santa Barbara
Santa Barbara, California

Written by Kate Sandoval

Edited by Kimberly Moore and Meryl Sustarsic

Layout by Meghan Dowdell

Additional contributions by Omid Gohari, Christina Koshzow, Chris Mason, Joey Rahimi, and Luke Skurman

ISBN # 1-4274-0161-6

Last updated 5/29/06

Special Thanks To: Babs Carryer, Andy Hannah, LaunchCyte, Tim O'Brien, Bob Sehlinger, Thomas Emerson, Andrew Skurman, Barbara Skurman, Bert Mann, Dave Lehman, Daniel Fayock, Chris Babyak, The Donald H. Jones Center for Entrepreneurship, Terry Slease, Jerry McGinnis, Bill Ecenberger, Idie McGinty, Kyle Russell, Jacque Zaremba, Larry Winderbaum, Roland Allen, Jon Reider, Team Evankovich, Lauren Varacalli, Abu Noaman, Mark Exler, Daniel Steinmeyer, Jared Cohon, Gabriela Oates, David Koegler, Glen Meakem, and the UC Santa Barbara Bounce-Back Team.

College Prowler®
5001 Baum Blvd.
Suite 750
Pittsburgh, PA 15213

Phone: 1-800-290-2682
Fax: 1-800-772-4972
E-mail: info@collegeprowler.com
Web Site: www.collegeprowler.com

How this all started...

When I was trying to find the perfect college, I used every resource that was available to me. I went online to visit school websites; I talked with my high school guidance counselor; I read book after book; I hired a private counselor. Sure, this was all very helpful, but nothing really told me what life was like at the schools I cared about. These sources weren't giving me enough information to be totally confident in my decision.

In all my research, there were only two ways to get the information I wanted.

The first was to physically visit the campuses and see if things were really how the brochures described them, but this was quite expensive and not always feasible. The second involved a missing ingredient: the students. Actually talking to a few students at those schools gave me a taste of the information that I needed so badly. The problem was that I wanted more but didn't have access to enough people.

In the end, I weighed my options and decided on a school that felt right and had a great academic reputation, but truth be told, the choice was still very much a crapshoot. I had done as much research as any other student, but was I 100 percent positive that I had picked the school of my dreams?

Absolutely not.

My dream in creating *College Prowler* was to build a resource that people can use with confidence. My own college search experience taught me the importance of gaining true insider insight; that's why the majority of this guide is composed of quotes from actual students. After all, shouldn't you hear about a school from the people who know it best?

I hope you enjoy reading this book as much as I've enjoyed putting it together. Tell me what you think when you get a chance. I'd love to hear your college selection stories.

Luke Skurman
CEO and Co-Founder
lukeskurman@collegeprowler.com

Welcome to College Prowler®

During the writing of College Prowler's guidebooks, we felt it was critical that our content was unbiased and unaffiliated with any college or university. We think it's important that our readers get honest information and a realistic impression of the student opinions on any campus—that's why if any aspect of a particular school is terrible, we (unlike a campus brochure) intend to publish it. While we do keep an eye out for the occasional extremist—the cheerleader or the cynic—we take pride in letting the students tell it like it is. We strive to create a book that's as representative as possible of each particular campus. Our books cover both the good and the bad, and whether the survey responses point to recurring trends or a variation in opinion, these sentiments are directly and proportionally expressed through our guides.

College Prowler guidebooks are in the hands of students throughout the entire process of their creation. Because you can't make student-written guides without the students, we have students at each campus who help write, randomly survey their peers, edit, layout, and perform accuracy checks on every book that we publish. From the very beginning, student writers gather the most up-to-date stats, facts, and inside information on their colleges. They fill each section with student quotes and summarize the findings in editorial reviews. In addition, each school receives a collection of letter grades (A through F) that reflect student opinion and help to represent contentment, prominence, or satisfaction for each of our 20 specific categories. Just as in grade school, the higher the mark the more content, more prominent, or more satisfied the students are with the particular category.

Once a book is written, additional students serve as editors and check for accuracy even more extensively. Our bounce-back team—a group of randomly selected students who have no involvement with the project—are asked to read over the material in order to help ensure that the book accurately expresses every aspect of the university and its students. This same process is applied to the 200-plus schools College Prowler currently covers. Each book is the result of endless student contributions, hundreds of pages of research and writing, and countless hours of hard work. All of this has led to the creation of a student information network that stretches across the nation to every school that we cover. It's no easy accomplishment, but it's the reason that our guides are such a great resource.

When reading our books and looking at our grades, keep in mind that every college is different and that the students who make up each school are not uniform—as a result, it is important to assess schools on a case-by-case basis. Because it's impossible to summarize an entire school with a single number or description, each book provides a dialogue, not a decision, that's made up of 20 different topics and hundreds of student quotes. In the end, we hope that this guide will serve as a valuable tool in your college selection process. Enjoy!

OMID GOHARI ◯ CHRISTINA KOSHZOW ◯ CHRIS MASON ◯ JOEY RAHIMI ◯ LUKE SKURMAN ◯
The College Prowler Team

Table of Contents

Introduction from the Author

Sun, waves, bikinis and board shorts, and incredible weather year-round make it hard not to mistake this school for some sort of twenty-something resort. But, then you realize that this resort offers great classes and boasts expert professors, and that the resort dwellers are actually serious students. UCSB is a place that offers both a strong academic and strong social side of the college experience. Students who are "go-getters" and good time-managers will thrive in this big-campus, opportunity-filled environment.

UCSB has begun to shy away from the "party-school" image that it has upheld for so many years. Both students and teachers are serious in their academic endeavors, and the media and applicants have started to notice. Three Nobel prizes have been awarded to UCSB professors in the last several years, the number of applicants has climbed and exceeded practically all of the other UC schools. Still, nobody, not even Chancellor Yang, can deny that UCSB maintains a thriving party scene. You will undoubtedly have many opportunities to be part of crazy Del Playa house parties and some downtown bar hopping.

When you fill out the University of California admission application, you choose which UC campus to apply to with a simple check in a box. I knew nothing about UCSB, but, since checking a box was probably the easiest part of college applications, I decided to apply to it along with the other UC schools I knew. A seemingly unimportant, even random, check has made the last four years the best years of my life. I know I had no idea if UCSB was the perfect school for me when I decided to come here; in fact, I don't think I knew it was the perfect school for me even after my first year. Eventually, I made friends, found inspiring professors, and took classes that I was really interested in. I explored Santa Barbara and beyond—I learned to surf (sort of), I interned, I volunteered, I worked, I played, and I soaked in plenty of Santa Barbara sun. UCSB has truly fulfilled all of my college expectations, and I'm already enjoying the benefits of my UCSB degree. Obviously I can't capture the exact life of every UCSB student, but hopefully this guidebook will present prospective students with some useful information about the school—both what it has to offer and, most importantly, what the environment is really like here. Have fun reading!

Kate Sandoval, Author
UC Santa Barbara

By the Numbers

General Information

UC Santa Barbara
552 University Rd.
Santa Barbara, CA 93106

Control:
Public

Academic Calendar:
Quarters

Religious Affiliation:
None

Founded:
1944 (became affiliated with
University of California)

Web Site:
www.ucsb.edu

Main Phone:
(805) 893-8000

Admissions Phone:
(805) 893-2881

Student Body

**Full-Time
Undergraduates:**
17,529

**Part-Time
Undergraduates:**
592

**Total Male
Undergraduates:**
8,091

**Total Female
Undergraduates:**
10,030

Admissions

Overall Acceptance Rate:
53%

Total Applicants:
36,963

Total Acceptances:
19,589

Freshman Enrollment:
3,898

Yield (% of admitted students
who actually enroll):
20%

Early Decision Available?
No

Early Action Available?
No

Regular Decision Deadline:
November 30

**Regular Decision
Notification:**
March 15

Must-Reply-By Date:
May 1

**Transfer Applications
Received:**
8,398

**Transfer Applicants
Accepted:**
5,624

Transfer Students Enrolled:
1,552

**Transfer Application
Acceptance Rate:**
67%

**Common Application
Accepted?**
No

Admissions E-Mail:
appinfo@sa.ucsb.edu

Admissions Web Site:
www.finaid.ucsb.edu

SAT I or ACT Required?
Either

**SAT I Range
(25th–75th Percentile):**
1070–1300

**SAT I Verbal Range
(25th–75th Percentile):**
520–640

**SAT I Math Range
(25th–75th Percentile):**
550–660

Retention Rate:
91%

**Top 10% of
High School Class:**
96%

Application Fee:
$40

Financial Information

Full-Time Tuition:
$6,952 in-state
$24,772 out-of-state

Room and Board:
$10,958

Books and Supplies:
$1,435 per year

**Average Need-Based
Financial Aid Package
(including loans, work-study,
grants, and other sources):**
$17,483

**Students Who Applied for
Financial Aid:**
61%

Students Who Received Aid:
49%

**Financial Aid Forms
Deadline:**
File FAFSA by March 3rd

*(FYI: The UCSB School Code
is 001320.)*

Financial Aid Phone:
(805) 893-2432

Financial Aid Web site:
www.finaid.ucsb.edu

Did You Know?

91 percent of freshmen return the next year.

Academics

The Lowdown On...
Academics

Degrees Awarded:
Bachelor
Certificate
Master
Doctorate

Most Popular Majors:
11% Business
8% Sociology
7% Psychology
6% International/Global
   Studies
5% Political Science and
   Government

Undergraduate Schools:
College of Letters and Science
College of Engineering
College of Creative Studies

Graduation Rates:
Four-year: 50%
Five-year : 72%
Six-year: 77%

→

Full-time Faculty:
919 (87%)

Faculty with Terminal Degree:
100%

Student-to-Faculty Ratio:
17:1

Average Course Load:
16 units
(usually about four classes)

Special Degree Options:
Create your own interdisciplinary studies major through the College of Letters and Science

AP Test Score Requirements
Possible credit for scores of 3, 4, and 5

Sample Academic Clubs
Debate Team, English Club, Philosophy Club, Regents and Chancellor's Scholarship Society, Accounting Club

Did You Know?

As a UCSB student, you have the opportunity to **spend a quarter in Washington DC** or at another UC campus through the UCDC program, and all of your units will transfer!

Best Places to Study:
University Center (UCEN), Library (8th floor reading room), Java Jones, Goleta Coffee Co., Santa Barbara Roasting Co., the beach

> "The classes offered are one of the reasons I chose to come here. Geological Catastrophes, Death and Dying, Vampirism, and Human Sexuality are as good as general education requirements get."

Q "Teachers vary depending on the major. For the most part, **every professor I've experienced has been really cooperative and understanding**. This is a fairly big University, so it can get intimidating, especially as a freshman when your classes tend to be bigger. Professors always have office hours, and TAs are always there to help; you just have to take the initiative and ask."

Q "Every teacher is different. If you want to have a relationship with your teacher, you pretty much need to seek them out, but they are very helpful in office hours. **You also have TAs that are pretty accessible**."

Q "The classes can be challenging, so you have to be able to apply yourself. There are plenty of opportunities to excel if you want to, in research, jobs, or clubs. But **the people here, I feel, are easier-going and less competitive**, so not everyone is out to kill just to make the grade. You just have to get your studies done first, and then find extra time to surf, hike, and lay out."

Q "There are a lot of good professors. **The classes themselves are large, so there isn't a lot of one-on-one contact**, but TAs help students out. Anyway, the professors are mostly pretty good—of course there are always those who aren't."

Q "There are many excellent professors at UCSB. In my department, **we have professors who are concerned with students' learning and enjoyment above all else**. There are, of course, strict and difficult professors, as well. Basically, it's up to the student to get to know their professor and get the most out of the class, and at UCSB, many undergraduates don't. Many have hard times in their classes and get poor grades because they don't try hard enough."

Q "UCSB has some of the worst undergraduates around. **I've seen many community-college students with more drive and dedication than the people here**. Now, there are those that try really hard, and subsequently do well. Unfortunately, this is a "party school," and it often lives up to its reputation. If you are serious about your classes, you can get a great education here, and work with some fantastic professors."

Q "I've done research with three different professors in my three years here, so **there are plenty of chances to work with faculty**, if that interests you. The school is also large enough so that, if you want, you can remain just a name, as well."

Q "The teachers here are much less pretentious than other more 'well-known' institutions. **They have a lot of respect for students and their ideas**. I feel that I can explore questions together with them. Often, the most interesting parts of the class are left out of the lecture in the interest of time, but they can be learned in office hours. My classes usually become most interesting when I'm applying the knowledge I just learned to the research lab, or even in another class, which is when I know I have really learned something important."

Q "My main piece of advice is to go to the classes you think you want the first week, and have some alternates so that if the teacher seems really bad, you can take the other class. It isn't worth it to take a class (as good as you think it will be) with a terrible teacher. **There are way too many good teachers and interesting classes on campus** to take something you just hate!"

Q "**Impacted majors have weeded-out classes that you have to take to get into the major**. Stick through them if you can, because the upper-division courses are much, much better. Some course listings have no course descriptions. Try to find out what the topics of these courses are by e-mailing the respective professors—the advanced seminars are usually some of the best classes."

Q "**In general, the UC system is very theory- and research-based**. For example, the communication major is more about research methods and interpersonal communication, not media. The drama department doesn't offer musical theatre. It focuses on classical training and theory."

Q "**UCSB is the secret spot for really amazing professors**, and their credentials prove it. I think the professors have figured out that Santa Barbara is a great place to live, and they can get paid while they are here."

The College Prowler Take On...
Academics

Although each department might have its monotone, sleep-inducing professor, most of the instructors are experts in their fields, excited about what they teach, and very accessible. UCSB is unique in that it has very few graduate students, so teachers are focused on their undergraduates. They have more time, teach almost all of the classes offered each quarter, and answer e-mails quickly. In the first two years of college, while people take their general education classes, they don't necessarily get to know the professors; lectures involve around 100 people and a teaching assistant runs the weekly section and grades. But classes later thin out to between 35-45 people as students advance in their majors.

The UCSB academic program has made a concerted effort to shed the "party-school" image and prove that the professors and students take academics very seriously. UCSB sometimes gets lost behind UCLA and Berkeley, but the latest statistics prove that Santa Barbara is working on a new reputation. The thing to realize about academics at UCSB, is that each student decides whether he or she is going to take the easy classes and never get to know the professors (which plenty of students do), or alternatively, help with research, take hard classes, and participate in the honors program. One of the reasons the student quotes are so varied is because there are a lot of partiers who do not go to class, and there are also a lot of serious students who spend most of their time studying and researching. It's up to you to decide how you will spend your time and what college life means to you.

The College Prowler® Grade on
Academics: B+

A high Academics grade generally indicates that Professors are knowledgeable, accessible, and genuinely interested in their students' welfare. Other determining factors include class size, how well professors communicate, and whether or not classes are engaging.

Local Atmosphere

The Lowdown On...
Local Atmosphere

Region:
West Coast

City, State:
Santa Barbara, CA

Setting:
Beach town

Distance from LA:
1 hour, 30 minutes

**Distance from
San Francisco:**
5 hours

**Distance from
Las Vegas:**
5 hours

Points of Interest:
Campus Point
The Mission
Santa Ynez Mountains
State Street
Stearn's Wharf

➡

Closest Shopping Malls:

Camino Real Marketplace
La Cumbre Mall
Paseo Nuevo Mall

Closest Movie Theaters:

The Arlington

(15 minutes from campus, but it has an old-fashioned screen)

1317 State St.

(805) 963-4408

Camino Real Theatre

(student discount on Tuesdays)

6950 Marketplace Dr., off of Storke Rd.

(805) 963-9503

Isla Vista Theatre

(shows $3 movies and sometimes pre-screenings)

UCSB
Embarcadero del Norte

Major Sports Teams:

Angels (hockey)

Clippers (basketball)

Dodgers (baseball)

Lakers (basketball)

LA Kings (hockey)

LA Sparks (basketball)

The Mighty Ducks (hockey) are in nearby Anaheim, about 25 miles South of LA

City Web Sites

www.santabarbaraca.com

www.newspress.com

www.independent.com

These links will give you all of the information and connecting links you need to keep up with local news, entertainment, and restaurant listings.

Did You Know?

Fun Facts about Santa Barbara:

- The **first Kinko's** was in Isla Vista, created by a UCSB grad student.
- **Big Dogs Brand, Patagonia**, and *Islands Magazine* all have their headquarters here.
- **JFK and new wife Jackie O.** finished off their honeymoon in Santa Barbara.
- The Santa Barbara **International Film Festival** and the Santa Barbara Writer's Conference are annual events.
- Santa Barbara County is **becoming one of the best wine-producing regions** on the coast.

Famous People Living in Santa Barbara:

Jennifer Aniston

Jeff Bridges

Julia Childs

John Cleese

Julia Louis-Dreyfus

"Bachelor" Andrew Firestone

Billy Idol

Kathy Ireland

Michael Keaton

Michael Jackson

Steve Martin

Brad Pitt

Ivan Reitman

Oprah Winfrey

Local Slang:

Hendry's – The beach that non-locals know as Arroyo Burro

Carp – Carpinteria, a beach town just south of Santa Barbara

State – State Street, where all the downtown shopping and dining is located

APS – Alameda Padre Serra, the street that cuts across the top of the foothills, or "Riviera," and has a great view of downtown and the ocean

Brooks – The photography institute in Montecito

RoCo – Santa Barbara Roasting Company, a downtown coffee shop

Students Speak Out On...
Local Atmosphere

> **"Isla Vista is probably one of the best college towns in the country."**

Q "**It's definitely a laid-back atmosphere—we live on the beach**. Isla Vista (IV) is a condensed square mile of college kids squished together. Santa Barbara City College is not far away, and a lot of kids who go there live in IV. Cal Poly San Luis Obispo is about an hour and a half north of here, and is pretty fun. Los Angeles is only an hour and a half south."

Q "**Isla Vista is a really mellow town** with a nice beach-bum feel to it. On a Saturday afternoon, we go play Frisbee, golf, or hang out. The nice thing about IV is that almost everyone you know lives within a square mile, so you can walk or bike to anyone's house in no time."

Q "If you can imagine a bunch of 20-year-olds hanging out together, that's basically the atmosphere here. It's **definitely very laid-back and has a party atmosphere**, but when you need to buckle down to study, it's possible. We also have a lot of Santa Barbara City College kids hanging out here, too, who are usually the non-stop partiers. It's a lot of fun, and the placement of the campus and the town couldn't be better. Downtown is about 10 minutes away, the mountains are 15 minutes away, and the beach is literally right next to campus. It's a great location; I couldn't ask for better."

Q "**Serious students avoid Isla Vista**, while the less academically-inclined seem to spend an inordinate amount of time there."

Q "**Avoid Isla Vista if you want to get good grades** and want to graduate in four years. Other than that, Goleta (where UCSB is located) is a decent little town, and Santa Barbara is a good-sized city."

Q "We live in one of the most beautiful places in the world. **The mountains and oceans are both right here**, and there is a lot less development than other cities in Southern California. There's so much stuff to do locally, and a lot of activism to get involved with."

Q "**Isla Vista is great for the first couple of years**, but don't miss out on all the stuff to do in downtown Santa Barbara, Santa Ynez, Summerland, and Carpinteria."

Q "At first, it seemed as if there was nothing to do here for free, but I proved myself wrong. There are tons of great day hikes in the mountains or around the beaches, a few free/cheap museums to explore, and weekend art walks and markets along the beach downtown. It's also **fun to visit Red Rock** when it's overcast in town, and Lake Cachuma."

Q "**Santa Barbara residents are, for the most part, very affluent**, which can actually be an advantage when you are a student who needs a good-paying job and some career connections!"

Q "After living in Isla Vista for a year, nothing will shock you. **The other day I saw my neighbor take his pet goat for a walk**—somehow, that is not weird to me."

The College Prowler Take On...
Local Atmosphere

Isla Vista, once deemed the "student ghetto" and patrolled by the National Guard in the 1960s, is a square-mile town right next to the campus. Most UCSB students live in Isla Vista and bike to campus everyday (a 10-minute bike ride, max). Around here, it's just called IV. The party street, Del Playa (DP), is on a cliff overlooking the ocean. Without a doubt, Isla Vista is one of the most unique and fun places most people will ever live. Where else can you choose from 10-30 parties on the weekend, hang out on the beach, and stand in line at four in the morning for burritos and pizza with hundreds of other college students?

The two beaches by Isla Vista are Devereux and Sands. If it's at all sunny, you can bet that both will be crowded with tanners and surfers (actually, the surfers are there no matter what the weather). The mountains are about a 15-minute drive away and provide plenty of opportunities for hiking. Isla Vista also has casual and inexpensive restaurants, and most do not close before 2 a.m. any night of the week. Just consider yourself warned that, with such a great atmosphere, productivity can be very low. Some students know that they will only stay focused if they live outside of Isla Vista.

B+

The College Prowler® Grade on

Local Atmosphere: B+

A high Local Atmosphere grade indicates that the area surrounding campus is safe and scenic. Other factors include nearby attractions, proximity to other schools, and the town's attitude toward students.

Safety & Security

The Lowdown On...
Safety & Security

Number of UCSB Police:
29

UCSB Police Phone:
(805) 893-3446

Safety Services:
Campus Security Officers (CSOs) are ready to escort you every night of the week. Just pick up a red phone on campus or call (805) 893-2000.

(Safety Services, continued)
The UC Police Department and paramedics are also on-call and patrolling 24 hours a day, 365 days of the year.

The Women's Center and Rape Prevention Services are easily accessible.

Health Services:

Student Health offers STD testing, immunizations, eye care, physical therapy, primary care, travel medicine, allergy shots, health advising, orthopedics, physicals, psychiatry, minor surgery, pharmacy, podiatry, rheumatology, women's health, x-ray, dermatology, and dental care. The Counseling Center also offers psychiatric services such as CAPS (Counseling and Psychological Services).

Health Clinic Hours:

Monday–Friday,
8 a.m.–4:30 p.m.

Did You Know?

You can register your bike with the Campus Security Officers. If your bike is stolen, they will attempt to find it for you—they have over a **30 percent recovery rate**, which is twice the US average.

Students Speak Out On...
Safety & Security

"Campus safety is good. We have campus security officers who patrol, and whom you can call for an escort if you need it."

Q "There have been issues recently with safety, especially my senior year, but I think that's common with any college. **I wouldn't worry about anything except maybe bike theft** . . . and damage you may cause yourself."

Q "I have never been concerned about safety, but then **things can happen on a big campus** anywhere."

Q "I feel very safe at UCSB. There are **foot-patrol officers all around Isla Vista**, and there are also student officers."

Q "The campus security is pretty good. **They have Campus Service Officers on duty 24 hours a day**. You can call them from the emergency phones located on campus."

Q "I suppose that security at UCSB is pretty good. The **campus has CSO officers, and they patrol the campus**. If it's late at night and you want someone to walk or bike you home, you can just give them a call and they will keep you company. I've never really used the service . . . but, there have not been many times when I didn't feel safe. Then again, I'm a guy and I do know that a lot of girls may not feel comfortable walking around on the streets at 2 a.m. with a bunch of drunken kids stumbling about."

Q "Security is good. It's important anywhere to walk in groups and make sure you are smart, but **the police are all over the place during the weekend**."

Q "Safety and security on campus seems to be really good.**I don't know of anybody who has had anything happen to them** while they were here, except a few who had their cars messed up by drunk students late at night."

Q "The campus security is really good as far as I'm concerned. **The lighting at night isn't wonderful in all locations**, but we have an escort service which runs all over campus and into Isla Vista."

Q "Campus safety is really great. Campus is honestly really laid-back, and **I have never felt threatened or anything**, alone or with a group."

The College Prowler Take On...
Safety & Security

Students say that the biggest safety issues at UCSB involve bike theft and vehicle vandalism, and that they are pleased with the visibility of on-campus security. Campus police and student CSOs (Campus Security Officers) patrol the campus every night and are always available to escort people after dark. Getting into a dorm, if you look like a college student, is definitely easy, but because of the dorm locations, non-students would very rarely be near dorms anyway.

Overall, the campus is a safe place, but the bordering town of Isla Vista can be a little more dangerous. The police report that bike and backpack theft are their two main problems on campus, and most arrests in Isla Vista are alcohol related. Almost all reports of sexual assault concern alcohol and an acquaintance. It's always good advice that nobody should walk alone late at night, here or at any other college. If you are concerned for your safety, you can take advantage of the many resources on campus. In general, almost all students feel safe, and the crime in Isla Vista is usually just drunk kids beating up cars and burning couches—yes, burning couches.

The College Prowler® Grade on
Safety & Security: A

A high grade in Safety & Security means that students generally feel safe, campus police are visible, blue-light phones and escort services are readily available, and safety precautions are not overly necessary.

Computers

The Lowdown On...
Computers

High-Speed Network?
Yes

Wireless Network?
Yes

Number of Labs:
18 (some are just for specific majors)

Different computer labs are available depending on your major. The labs have fairly erratic hours, and schedules for each one can be found at *www.ic.ucsb.edu.*

(Computer Labs, continued)
Instructional Computing Labs are open-access labs for all students, unless a class has reserved the lab. There are at least 25 computers in each lab. All have at least 17" color monitors, black and white or color printing, Intel Pentium IV Processors, CD-ROM drive. Almost all have headphones and sound cards. Most have zip drives.

→

(Computer Labs, continued)

Ellison Lab: Ellison Hall 2626, 27 Dells, 8 Macs

Gaviota Lab: Phelps 1529, 25 Dells

HSSB Lab: Humanities and Social Sciences Building, Room 1203, 33 Dells, 7 Macs, Multimedia room, GIS room

Jalama Lab: Phelps 1517, 25 PowerMac Dual G4-450s

Language Lab: Kerr 2160, 31 PowerMac G4-350s

Leadbetter Lab: Phelps 1530, 25 Dells

Media Lab: Kerr 2160, 27 PowerMacs G4-350s

Mesa Lab: Phelps 1525, 25 Dells

Miramar Lab: Phelps 1526, 25 Dells

Open Access Lab: Phelps 1513, 16 PCs, 2 Macs

Rincon Lab: Phelps 1518, 25 Microns

Engineering Computer Labs:

Engineering Computer Labs are only available to Engineering students. They have a College of Engineering e-mail, web storage, disk space, and free printing for 200 pages per quarter. They are open until 2 a.m.

Engineering 1 Lab: Engineering 1 Building, Room 1140

Engineering 2 Lab: Engineering 2 Building, Room 3236

CAD Lab: Engineering 2 Building, Room 2223

CSIL Lab: Engineering 1 Building, Room 1138

Operating Systems:
PC and Mac

Number of Computers:
There are at least 18 computers in each lab

Discounted Software

(For a complete list, go to *www.ic.ucsb.edu* and click on "software library.") List includes: Microsoft Access, Adobe Acrobat, Adobe Acrobat Professional, Adobe After Effects, Macromedia Authorware, Macromedia ColdFusion MX, Adobe Creative Suites, Macromedia Director MX, Macromedia Dreamweaver MX, Microsoft Encarta, Microsoft Excel, FileMaker Pro Advanced, Macromedia Fireworks, Macromedia Flash, Adobe FrameMaker, Microsoft FrontPage, Adobe Illustrator, Microsoft Office XP, Adobe PageMaker, Microsoft PowerPoint, Microsoft Publisher, Microsoft Word

Charge to Print?

Yes, in most labs it is 15 cents per page, charged to your school account, unless you go to a lab that is sponsored by your major (such as the Engineering labs).

Did You Know?

 Check with your department about the computer labs and privileges that are open to you through your major.

Students Speak Out On...
Computers

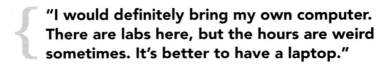

"I would definitely bring my own computer. There are labs here, but the hours are weird sometimes. It's better to have a laptop."

Q "**All of the dorms are wired**. There are a few open-access labs, and I have never had a problem getting into one if I needed to. Bringing a computer is a lot more convenient, but if you can't do it now, I wouldn't sweat it too much."

Q "On campus, **the computer network is awesome**. We have 20 megabytes of bandwidth for 1,800 students. It's very fast—faster than DSL or cable. Everyone brings their own computer. It's not necessary, but it is convenient. There are computer labs in each dorm. I didn't bring one originally. I got a computer loan because I was a little low on cash."

Q "**Computer labs are around and usually available**; however, you will want to bring one because they close early. It's much easier to have your own."

Q "You can access computers almost anywhere and get online. I would say that **the campus is well-connected**—not just in the labs but also in the offices, University Center, and the library."

Q "You should **definitely bring your own computer**. There are computer labs, but life is much, much easier if you have your own computer."

Q "**Engineering students have access to five computer labs** (open 8 a.m.–2 a.m.), which recently recieved new computers. They are also updated monthly with the latest versions of engineering programs. Every engineering student has memory on the X drive, which can be accessed from any of the engineering labs on campus."

Q "The computer network is pretty decent, **but it does get crowded sometimes**. I would definitely bring a computer, if that's an option for you."

Q "UCSB is fairly well wired, with **access ports in every dorm room, library, and building**. I would definitely suggest bringing your own computer, as many classes, campus offices, and services have materials on the Web."

Q "One of the questions I had before college was whether I should buy a laptop or a desktop. Although either type is fine, I really appreciate my laptop. Considering I moved every year of college, went home for breaks, and studied abroad, **the flexibility and simple packing of my laptop was really nice**. And taking my laptop to the coffee shop to study was an added benefit."

The College Prowler Take On...
Computers

UCSB campus computers are updated regularly. They have both Mac and PC computers with all the latest software and several printing options, in labs located across the campus. It's pretty easy to stop into a lab, either associated with your department or an open-access lab (Kerr Hall or Phelps Hall have the two biggest), to check your e-mail or print out a paper. Labs are a bit hidden on campus, though, so make sure to pay attention during your campus tour!

Even though the University has computer labs scattered around campus, the dorms all have Ethernet connections, so bring your own computer if you can. Students agree that relying on the campus computers is definitely feasible, but labs are not always accessible, or open all night, and can be crowded during peak study weeks. Compared to some other universities, UCSB does not have a sparkling, new computer everywhere you look, but you can find one to use if you need to. Most people do own their own computer, and particularly during their freshman year, spend hours a day instant messaging with friends, writing papers, doing Internet research for classes, and checking e-mail. It's very convenient to spend those hours at home instead of in a lab every day, especially since no one will notice if you do your work in your underwear with cheese-curl crumbs all over your shirt.

The College Prowler® Grade on

Computers: B

A high grade in Computers designates that computer labs are available, the computer network is easily accessible, and the campus' computing technology is up-to-date.

Facilities

The Lowdown On...
Facilities

Student Center:
The University Center (UCen) has fast food, a deli, a salad bar, and a coffee house, along with the Bookstore, Post Office, a computer lab, and plenty of couches to sleep, study, or hang out on. It also has the Corner Store, a convenience store that is best known for its huge selection of bin candy.

Libraries:
Davidson Library is the main library. It has eight floors and 2.6 million volumes, along with the necessary computers and copy machines. Don't expect it to be pretty; the library is definitely one of the ugliest buildings on campus—it's almost as if UCSB never wanted students to study.

The Arts Library is much smaller and located in the Music Building.

→

Athletic Center:
The Recreation Center (Rec Cen) is beautiful, with two outdoor pools, indoor and outdoor basketball courts, three weight rooms, cardio equipment, tennis and squash courts, a climbing wall, a roller hockey floor, and a Jacuzzi.

Popular Places to Chill:
Outside by the Campus Lagoon, or on the grass by the Arbor

Campus Size:
989 acres

What Is There to Do on Campus?
A lot of students will shop for shoes, paperbacks, posters, and jewelry at the outside stands in front of the University Center. Or students will walk through the University Art Museum or just take a nap by the Campus Lagoon.

Movie Theater on Campus?
No

Bar on Campus?
No, but the Hub, which is on ground floor of the University Center, has a couple of eateries that serve alcohol. The closest real bar is the Study Hall in Isla Vista.

Coffeehouse on Campus?
Yes, there is Nicoletti's in the University Center, and the Coral Tree Café by the Student Affairs building.

Facilities vs. The Other Campus Buildings
The UCen and Rec Cen are relatively new—some students say that those buildings were major draws for them to come to school here, but the other buildings range from 70s-inspired to state-of-the-art. The main problem is that none of the buildings match. The University has repainted all of the buildings and is working hard to update the older ones. The Bren Graduate School building is one of the only buildings in the nation to be ranked as a platinum-level environmentally-safe building.

Students Speak Out On...
Facilities

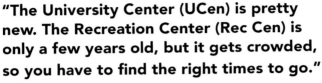

"The University Center (UCen) is pretty new. The Recreation Center (Rec Cen) is only a few years old, but it gets crowded, so you have to find the right times to go."

Q "**Everything is fairly clean**. There's not too much to complain about."

Q "The sports facility on campus has good equipment, but it can get really crowded. The **UCen is pretty cool; they have all the usual stuff**: post office, places to eat, bookstore, and copy place. They also have concerts in the Hub, located on the bottom floor of the UCen."

Q "Because everybody here is a fitness freak, **there are always tons of people at the gym**. There are lots of nice places to study or lounge both inside and outside. There are plenty of food options and stores. Some of the buildings are newer, so they're in nice shape."

Q "The **facilities here are pretty good**. They opened up a new gym in the last several years; I go there all the time."

Q "**The Rec Center on campus is free**, so that's always good. There are lots of classes and sports that take place there. You can get credit for classes like scuba diving and sailing through the Rec Center."

Q "**There are great athletic facilities that are pretty up-to-date**. The UCen is also great and usually busy."

Q "The facilities on campus are a little older, but they serve their purpose. We have a **really nice Recreation Center** with a workout area and large swimming pool. We also have indoor basketball and volleyball areas."

Q "Facilities on campus are pretty good. **The athletic ones are subpar** in my opinion, but the University Center and Recreation Center are really nice."

Q "The UCen and Rec Cen stand out, however, the **library could really use some improvements** aesthetically—orange floors and dark-brown wood siding were "out" a long time ago. Another comment is that none of the buildings match."

Q "**The University Center and the Recreation Center are beautiful**. Luckily, they recently expanded the Rec Cen. It still gets crowded, so I can only imagine how busy it used to be."

The College Prowler Take On...
Facilities

Although the library looks like it's from the Nixon era, other facilities are modern and more pleasing to the eye. UCSB has the Recreation Center (Rec Cen) that is free to all students and includes an outside lap and recreation pool, four inside basketball courts, racquetball courts, soccer fields, three weight rooms, cardio equipment, a climbing wall, a roller hockey floor, and a Jacuzzi. The floors and pools are well maintained, and the machines are updated. But, because it's so nice, it can be crowded to the point where, after waiting in line for an hour for your favorite elliptical machine, you just end up skipping the workout to meet your friends for food instead.

The University Center (UCen) is the student center that houses fast food restaurants, cafés with salad, pasta, pizza, and sandwiches, a coffee shop, the bookstore, and a computer lab. It's a favorite place to waste an hour while waiting for a class, offering students the chance to sleep, read the *Daily Nexus* on a couch, or check their e-mail. Students can also be spotted eating an inexpensive lunch, or grabbing a coffee or bin candy for some fuel to get through their next class. Students like the new, clean facilities, and use them daily—the only major complaints are the crowded Rec Center and the not-so-attractive library.

B+

The College Prowler® Grade on

Facilities: B+

A high Facilities grade indicates that the campus is aesthetically pleasing and well maintained, facilities are state-of-the-art, and libraries are exceptional. Other determining factors include the quality of both athletic and student centers and an abundance of things to do on campus.

Campus Dining

The Lowdown On...
Campus Dining

Freshman Meal Plan Requirement?
No

Meal Plan Average Cost:
$2,300 per year

Places to Grab a Bite with Your Meal Plan:
You can put money on your Access Card and use it everywhere on-campus, as well as the UCSB aquired housing buildings which are located as far as a mile away from campus.

Dining Commons:

Students choose a meal plan of either 14 or 19 meals per week and can eat at any of the dining halls. Take-out meals, cultural food events, nutrition classes, vegan, vegetarian, organic and low fat options are also offered.

Carrillo Dining Commons

Carillo offers students indoor and outdoor tables and different food stations such as a salad bar, grill, Mongolian line (which specializes in stir-fries), and an "oven" section that has freshly made pizzas and desserts.

De La Guerra Dining Commons

Possibly the biggest of UCSB's dining halls, De La Guerra was most recently renovated and offers the usual food stations, its specialty being a taco station.

Francisco Torres Dining Commons

Bought by the University from private ownership in 2003, Francisco Torres features a salad bar, hot line, grill, deli bar, desserts, beverage bar, and a specialty bar that is usually made-to-order Mexican or stir-fry. Vegetarian, vegan, and even organic options are offered.

Ortega Dining Commons

Ortega is a smaller dining area which offers salads, a hot food line, deserts, and a "sushi machine" which makes supposedly perfect sushi rolls.

Dining Units:

The Arbor

Food: Convenience store

Location: Across from main library

Favorite Dish: Coffee, espresso and candy

Hours: Monday–Thursday 7:30 a.m.–10 p.m., Friday 7:30 a.m.–4 p.m., Saturday 10 a.m.–3 p.m., Sunday 10 a.m.–9 p.m.

Chilitos

Food: Original Fresh-Mex

Location: Hub

Favorite Dish: Fajita burritos

Hours: Monday–Thursday 10:30 a.m.–6 p.m., Friday 10:30 a.m.–5 p.m., Saturday 11 a.m.–2 p.m.

Chilitos Express

Food: Fresh-Mex

Location: UCen

Favorite Dish: Taco salad, chicken burrito

Hours: Monday-Friday 11 a.m.-2 p.m.

The Coral Tree Café

Food: Traditional breakfasts and sandwiches

Location: near Cheadle Hall, about a 10-minute walk from UCen

Favorite Dish: Breakfast Burrito

Hours: Monday–Friday 7:30 a.m.–5 p.m.

The Corner Store

Food: Convenience shop with a wide variety of snacks

Location: Upstairs UCen

Favorite Dish: Candy

Hours: Monday–Thursday 7:30 a.m.–11 p.m., Friday 7:30 a.m.–7 p.m., Saturday 10 a.m.–6 p.m., Sunday 11 a.m.–8 p.m.

Die Bretzel

Food: Gourmet hot dogs and pretzels

Location: UCen cart

Favorite Dish: German sausage sandwich with sauerkraut

Hours: Monday–Friday 10 a.m.–3 p.m.

Gaucho Deli & Café

Food: Italian and Greek specialties. Dine in or out.

Location: Upstairs UCen

Favorite Dish: Chicken salad sandwich

Hours: Monday–Friday 7:30 a.m.–5 p.m.

Jamba Juice

Food: Smoothies and shakes

Location: Upstairs UCen

Favorite Dish: Mango-A-Go-Go, Protein Berry Pizzazz

Hours: Monday–Friday 7:30 a.m.–6 p.m., Saturday–Sunday 11 a.m.–4 p.m.

Nicoletti's Coffeehouse

Food: Specialty coffees, espressos, baked goods, and fresh fruit

Location: Upstairs UCen

Favorite Dish: Bagel and coffee

Hours: Monday–Thursday 7:30 a.m.–1 a.m., Friday 7:30 a.m.–7:30 p.m., Saturday 11 a.m.–3 p.m., Sunday 6 p.m.–1 a.m.

Nic's Northwest/Nic Too

Food: Coffee cart

Location: Both in UCen

Favorite Dish: Cup of joe

Hours: Monday–Friday 8 a.m.–3 p.m. Nic Too opened from 8 a.m.–4 p.m.

Panda Express

Food: Mandarin-style Chinese

Location: Hub

Favorite Dish: Orange-flavored chicken and chicken eggroll

(Panda Express, continued)

Hours: Monday–Thursday
10:30 a.m.–8 p.m.,
Friday 10:30 a.m.–7 p.m.,
Saturday 11 a.m.–5 p.m.

Pateró

Food: Pasta with homemade
sauces, daily specials and
famous homemade
cheese bread

Location: Upstairs UCen

Favorite Dish: Margarita,
palmero, pesto chicken, or
BBQ chicken pizza

Hours: Monday–Thursday
10:30 a.m.–6 p.m.,
Friday 10:30 a.m.–4 p.m.

Romaine's

Food: 26-foot salad bar
with vegetables, fresh fruit,
homemade soups, fresh
breadsticks, and muffins

Location: Upstairs UCen

Favorite Dish: Salad
and breadstick

Hours: Monday–Friday
10:30 a.m.–4 p.m

The Store at Buchanan

Food: Convenience store and
coffee cart

Location: Right outside of
Buchanan Hall

Favorite Dish: Coffee
and bagel

Hours: Monday–Thursday
7:30 a.m.–7 p.m.,
Friday 7:30 a.m.–4 p.m.

Wendy's

Food: Old-fashioned burgers

Location: Hub

Favorite Dish: Anything off
the dollar menu

Hours: Monday–Thursday
10 a.m.–8 p.m.,
Friday 10 a.m.–7 p.m.,
Saturday–Sunday
11 a.m.–5 p.m.

Off-Campus Places to Use Your Meal Plan:

None

24-Hour On-Campus Eating?

No

Student Favorites:

Gaucho Deli & Café

Jamba Juice

Nicoletti's

Panda Express

Romaine's

Did You Know?

Bin candy is the top seller at the Corner Store on campus and at the market in Isla Vista. **Sour Patch Kids is the top choice**.

Jack Johnson (UCSB graduate) sings about his dining hall "the DLG" (stands for De La Guerra) in his song "Bubble Toes."

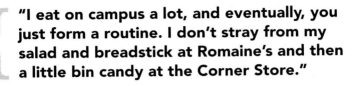

"I eat on campus a lot, and eventually, you just form a routine. I don't stray from my salad and breadstick at Romaine's and then a little bin candy at the Corner Store."

Q "The food is good. In the dorms, **you will get tired of the food no matter what**. It just gets old. We have De La Guerra (DLG), a student cafeteria where a lot of kids living on campus eat. In the University Center (UCen) there's a Wendy's, a Panda Express, a Mexican place, and a deli."

Q "I have a meal plan on campus. **I eat at the dinning commons and think the food is awesome**. People sometimes complain about it, but trust me, it's better than the cooking of anybody I know. They also have fast food places on campus."

Q "**The food on campus is alright**. We have your fast foods, but we also have a pizza place, salad buffet, deli, and Mexican restaurant."

Q "I lived in the on-campus dorms my first year. When doing so, you can go to any one of the different cafeterias. **The food is decent for a cafeteria**. At least they always have a salad bar; that's hard to ruin."

Q "Food on campus is okay. If you are a freshman, you will probably eat at the campus dining commons. It's buffet-style, but I really didn't like it. **The alternative is to pay for meals**."

Q "I didn't even buy a meal plan. **Any mass-produced food is bound to not be good**. If you don't want to gain the Freshman 15, then the dorm food isn't going to help."

Q "Food is good on campus. The dorms are not so good, but the restaurants themselves are yummy! We have this **really good sandwich place in the UCen called Gaucho Deli & Café**. That's my highlight."

Q "**I suggest the Coral Tree Café for on-campus food** because it isn't crowded and it has nice outside tables and good breakfasts."

Q "**Food on campus is good**, but the best places are off campus in Isla Vista."

Q "**The campus dining halls are scary**. Avoid them especially at the end of the week, when the week's leftovers are combined to make new treats."

Q "The food in the dining commons is pretty standard cafeteria food. **It gets old, but it's not that bad**."

Q "**The dorm food is pretty good**, but you tend to get tired of it by the end of the year."

The College Prowler Take On...
Campus Dining

Students say that the dorm food doesn't make them gag, but that it does become boring fairly quickly. Most enjoy eating in the on-campus restaurants instead, where the variety ranges from fast food to more café-like food and deli standards. Even the drinks are varied, with everything from coffee and frappuccinos to frozen juice drinks at Jamba Juice. Everyone seems to have their favorite place to recommend, like Romaine's for salads, Gaucho Deli for sandwiches, and The Coral Tree Café for a good breakfast. Currently, the Die Bretzel and Chilitos Express stands in the centrally-located Arbor are popular stops.

The dorm cafeterias do have one advantage—they offer vegan and vegetarian options. Francisco Torres used to be known as having the best dorm food because it was privately owned, had the best hours, and offered an unlimited meal plan. But now that UCSB has bought Francisco Torres, the food has become more like the on-campus food, yet continues to offer some of the extras that it used to. All of the dorm cafeterias have a salad bar, a grill, frozen yogurt, a hot-food line, and the staples for making a decent deli sandwich. Despite the fact that the food gets boring and isn't always very healthy or gourmet, dorm food is bearable for a year. If your tastes run similar to most of the students around here, you're going to want to stock up on your Access Card, which you can use at any of the on-campus restaurants.

The College Prowler® Grade on
Campus Dining: C+

Our grade on Campus Dining addresses the quality of both school-owned dining halls and independent on campus restaurants as well as the price, availability, and variety of food available.

Off-Campus Dining

The Lowdown On...
Off-Campus Dining

Restaurant Prowler:
Popular Places to Eat!

Bagel Café
Food: Bagels and coffee
6551 Trigo Rd.
(805) 685-7114
Cool Features: Good bagel melts and sandwiches
Price: $1–$5
Hours: Daily 6 a.m.–4 p.m.

Brophy Brothers
Food: Seafood
119 Harbor Way
(805) 966-4418

(Brophy Brothers, continued)
Cool Features: Great view overlooking the water.
Price: $10–$20
Hours: Sunday–Thursday 11 a.m.–10 p.m., Friday–Saturday 11 a.m.–11 p.m.

Cajun Kitchen
Food: Breakfast and Creole
6831 Hollister Ave.
(805) 683-8864
Cool Features: Louisiana-style cuisine
Price: $6–$12
Hours: Daily 6:30 a.m.–2:30 p.m.

Cajun Kitchen Café
Food: Breakfast and Cajun
1924 De La Vina
(805) 687-2062
Cool Features: Coupons
offered at:
www.cajunkitchensb.com
Price: $4–$8
Hours: Daily 6:30 a.m.–
2:30 p.m.

The Cantina
Food: Mexican
966 Embarcadero del Mar
(805) 968-2862
Cool Features: Best breakfast
burritos
Price: $4–$8
Hours: Daily 8:30 a.m.–10 p.m.

China Pavilion - Montecito
Food: Chinese
1070 Coast Village Rd.
(805) 565-9380
Cool Features: Trendy
atmosphere
Price: $10–$20
Hours: Monday–Saturday
11:30 a.m.–3 p.m.,
5:30–9:30 p.m.,
Sunday 5:30–9:30 p.m.

Deja Vu
Food: American
966 Embarcadero del Mar
(805) 968-8888
Cool Features: Delivery service
Price: $2–$8
Hours: Daily 11 a.m.–1 a.m.

Freebirds World Burrito
Food: Mexican
879 Embarcadero del Norte
(805) 968-0123
Cool Features: Huge burritos,
All-you-can-eat contests
Price: $4–$7
Hours: Daily 24 hours

Giovanni's
Food: Pizza, pasta, sandwiches
6583 Pardall Rd.
(805) 968-2254
Cool Features: common
meeting place
Price: $4–$10
Hours: Daily 11 a.m.–11 p.m.

The Habit
Food: Hamburgers
5735 Hollister Ave.
(805) 964-0366
Cool Features: 100% lean
meat, bread baked fresh
daily, milkshakes use real ice
cream, fries made with 100%
vegetable oil
Price: $3–$7
Hours: Daily 11 a.m.–10 p.m.

Javan's
Food: Sandwiches, grill
938 Embarcadero del Norte
(805) 968-2180
Cool Features: $2 hamburgers
Price: $2–$5
Hours: Daily 11 a.m.–11 p.m.

The Natural Café
Food: Sandwiches, salads, and soups
5892 Hollister Ave.
(805) 692-2363
Cool Features: Healthy
Price: $4–$10
Hours: Sunday–Thursday
11 a.m.–9 p.m.,
Friday–Saturday
11 a.m.–10 p.m.

The Palace Grill
Food: Cajun and Creole
8 E. Cota St
(805) 963-5000
Cool Features: Great food without pretense; tamborine-playing dancers perform while guests wait to be seated.
Price: $10–$20
Hours: Sunday–Thursday
11 a.m.–3 p.m., 5:30–10 p.m.,
Friday–Saturday
11 a.m.–3 p.m., 5:30–11 p.m.

Palazzio
Food: Italian
1026 State St.
(805) 564-1985
Cool Features: family-style portions
Price: $10–$20
Hours: Daily 11:30 a.m.–3 p.m., Sunday–Thursday
5:30–11 p.m.,
Friday–Saturday
5:30 p.m.–12 a.m.

Sam's To Go
Food: Subs
6560 Pardall Rd.
(805) 685-8895
Cool Features: Outdoor patio great for people-watching
Price: $3–$6
Hours: Daily 10 a.m.–11 p.m.

Silvergreens
Food: Salad, soup, sandwiches
900 Embarcadero del Mar
(805) 961-1700
Cool Features: You can order smaller portions of combined menu items (half & half and threesome orders).
Price: $4–$10
Hours: Daily 11 a.m.–1 a.m.

Sushi Teri
Food: Japanese Grill and sushi
909 Embarcadero del Mar
(805) 685-4822
Cool Features: Take-out
Price: $4–$12
Hours: Monday–Saturday
11:30 a.m.–2 p.m.,
5 p.m.–9:30 p.m.

Woodstock's
Food: Pizza
928 Embarcadero del Norte
(805) 968-6969
Cool Features: Cinnabread
Price: $5–$13
Hours: Sunday–Thursday
11 a.m.–12 a.m.,
Friday–Saturday 11 a.m.–1 a.m.

Closest Grocery Stores:

Isla Vista Market
939 Embarcadero del Mar
(805) 968-3597

Mac's Market
915 Embarcadero del Mar
(805) 968-1316

24-Hour Eating:

Freebirds World Burrito

Student Favorites:

Freebirds World Burrito,
Silvergreens, Woodstock's,

Late-Night, Half-Price Food Specials:

Silvergreens

Best Pizza:

Woodstock's, Giovanni's

Best Chinese:

China Pavilion - Montecito

Best Breakfast:

Bagel Café, Cajun Kitchen

Best Healthy:

Silvergreens,
The Natural Café

Best Place to Take Your Parents:

Palazzio, The Palace Grille,
Brophy Brothers

Did You Know?

The Web site, *www.nippers.com*, has many good
Santa Barbara restaurant reviews, as well
as *www.diningsantabarbara.com* and
www.santabarbara.com. Despite Santa Barbara's
population, there are **hundreds of restaurants
to try**.

A version of Shepherd's Salad was invented in Santa Barbara;
in fact, you can meet Mr. Shepherd at his farmer's market stand
on Saturday mornings.

Anything called "local's favorite" or "Santa Barbara style" will
include **avocado and sprouts**.

Every year, Goleta has a lemon festival, Carpinteria has an
avocado festival, and Oxnard has a strawberry festival.

Students Speak Out On...
Off-Campus Dining

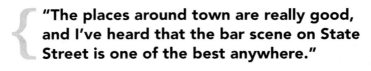

"The places around town are really good, and I've heard that the bar scene on State Street is one of the best anywhere."

Q "They have great food places. **My personal favorite is Freebirds World Burrito**; it's the best Mexican place I know. It's on Embarcadero del Norte."

Q "Close to Isla Vista, where you will most likely live after your first year, there are some great places to eat. In Goleta, there is **a good burger place called the Habit on Hollister**; on Calle Real and Embarcadero del Mar there are Sushi Teri Japanese restaurants. There's also a lot of really nice places on State Street downtown."

Q "There are some pretty decent places to eat in Isla Vista. There's also many types of fast food. Woodstock's and Giovanni's have good pizza and Italian food. **Cantina has Mexican food, but isn't that great**. All of the freshmen eat at Freebirds World Burrito, which is a fast food Mexican place, but most people get sick of it pretty quickly. Finally, Silvergreens is a good sandwich and salad place."

Q "There are many restaurants off campus. **Many are expensive because of our location in Santa Barbara**. Places in the neighborhood like Freebirds World Burrito, Woodstock's, and Silvergreens are commonplace for everyone, but they seem to easily bore everyone."

Q "If you go off campus and into Isla Vista, there are **bunches of places to go**. There are sandwich places, pizza places, Asian places, and Mexican places."

Q "Off campus in Isla Vista there are a bunch of good places—**Woodstock's for pizza, Freebirds World Burritos for burritos, Sam's for subs, and Silvergreens for salads**. There are also tons of food places in Goleta, but that is a 5-10 minute drive. The food places in IV are a walk from campus, or a bike ride away."

Q "Off campus, like two to four blocks away, are plenty of pizza (Woodstock's is the best) and sandwich places. **Everything seems to be pretty expensive**. Santa Barbara is one of the wealthiest areas around, so bring money."

Q "You can't find a better place to eat than Santa Barbara. **Downtown has millions of great restaurants** like Palazzio's, and Brophy Brothers."

Q "The food in Santa Barbara and Goleta is awesome. Your only decision will be which place to eat. Isla Vista has some legendary and great quick-eat places. Goleta has some great finds, too. **If you like good Mexican food or sushi, you'll be in heaven in this town**."

Q "The restaurants in Isla Vista and downtown are great. There's a lot of variety and some wonderful places to choose from. Just about all the little places in IV are worth going to at least once, and most of them I am going to dearly miss once I move away. **Bagel Café and Silvergreen's are two of the best**. When the parents come to visit, there are great places on the harbor and pier downtown."

The College Prowler Take On...
Off-Campus Dining

This tourist city has anything that you might crave—and then some. In Isla Vista, go to Freebirds for 24-hour Mexican food or to Woodstock's for unique pizza concoctions that everyone loves. Cantina is the best for breakfast burritos—even locals like Brad Pitt know that. Students enjoy the variety and the quality of restaurants in Isla Vista. Many say that there are good Mexican and Italian places in abundance, and plenty of spots to get good sushi. They also mention how easy it is to find a restaurant that serves healthy food, like Silvergreens.

Goleta, the city that encompasses Isla Vista, features a couple of good restaurants such as the Habit, a good and greasy hamburger and milkshake place, or the Natural Café, an inexpensive and healthy restaurant. Santa Barbara, which is about a 10-minute drive from campus, has what seems like a million restaurants to choose from. A good place to go for a dinner that's under $25 a person is the Palace Grill on the Harbor. This modest list just scratches the surface of all of the great restaurants to try, but the downside is that Santa Barbara is very expensive. You can get away with less than $10 for dinner in Isla Vista, but plan on at least $20 downtown. After four years, I don't think anyone can claim that they have tried all the restaurants here.

A-

The College Prowler® Grade on

Off-Campus Dining: A-

A high Off-Campus Dining grade implies that off-campus restaurants are affordable, accessible, and worth visiting. Other factors include the variety of cuisine and the availability of alternative options (vegetarian, vegan, kosher, etc.)

Campus Housing

The Lowdown On...
On-Campus Housing

Room Types:
There are three, four, and five-person suites with a shared bathroom, or two-person rooms with a hall bathroom that about 50 students share. All dorms are coed, but some floors are single-sex. A few singles exist, but they are hard to come by. Campus has room for 4,700 students to live on campus.

Best Dorms:
Manzanita Village

Worst Dorms:
San Rafael (it's mostly transfer students or upperclassmen)

Number of Dormitories:
10 (8 where freshmen live)

Number of University-Owned Apartments:
3

Undergrads Living on Campus:
5,083 (29%)

Dormitories

Anacapa Hall

Floors: 2

Total Occupancy: 100

Bathrooms: 1 single-gendered restroom per 25-40 residents

Coed: Yes, men and women reside in adjacent wings on each floor

Room Types: Doubles

Special Features: Close to outdoor patio, volleyball nets, and ocean

Fontainebleu

Floors: 3

Total Occupancy: 255 spaces in the Main facility, which borders directly on the campus at the west gate to the University, and 175 spaces in the Annex facility, which is two blocks west at 811 Camino Pescadero.

Bathrooms: 2 per 5 residents

Coed: Yes

Room Types: Suites with 3 bedrooms, one double one triple

Special Features: University-affiliated, privately-owned and operated, scheduled housekeeping service, pool, full-service meals, Ethernet Internet, and cable TV, laundry facilities, recreation room, computer room, and permit parking

Francisco Torres

Floors: 8 floors, 2 towers

Total Occupancy: 480

Bathrooms: 1 bathroom between 2 suites

Coed: Yes

Room Types: Suites, all doubles

Special Features: Sinks in rooms, swimming pool, volleyball, basketball, and tennis courts

Manzanita Village

Floors: 3–4 floor towers, in 17 buildings

Total Occupancy: 800

Bathrooms: 1 per 4 residents

Coed: Yes

Room Types: Suites, doubles and singles

Special Features: Opened in 2002, ocean views, Carrillo Dining Commons, courtyard

San Miguel

Floors: 2 towers, each 8 floors

Total Occupancy: 800

Bathrooms: 1 single-gender restroom per 25 residents

Coed: Yes, men and women housed on alternating floors

Room Types: Doubles and singles

Special Features: Closest to the University Center, theme floors

San Nicolas

Floors: 8, "L-shaped" tower

Total Occupancy: 400

Bathrooms: 1 single-gendered restroom per 25 residents

Coed: Yes, men and women housed on separate wings of each floor

Room Types: Doubles, some singles

Special Features: Houses the Resident Hall Headquarters, computer lab

San Rafael

Floors: 3 floors, 2 buildings

Total Occupancy: 250

Bathrooms: 1 single-gendered restroom per 4–10 residents

Coed: Yes, men and women are housed in alternating suites

Room Types: Varies; singles, doubles, or suites for 4 or 8 residents

Special Features: Primarily for transfer students, Carrillo Dining Commons, courtyard

Santa Cruz

Floors: 2

Total Occupancy: 100

Bathrooms: 1 single-gender restroom per 25-40 residents

Coed: Yes, men and women reside in adjacent wings

Room Types: Doubles

Special Features: Interest floors are substance free and multicultural, close to campus point beach

Santa Rosa

Floors: 2

Total Occupancy: 60-100

Bathrooms: 1 single-gendered restroom per 25-40 residents

Coed: Yes, men and women housed in adjacent wings

Room Types: Doubles

Special Features: Closest to center of campus, fitness center and game room, Carrillo Dining Commons

Tropicana Gardens

Floors: 2

Total Occupancy: 460

Bathrooms: 2 bathrooms per 5 residents or 1 bathroom per 3 residents

Coed: Yes

Room Types: 3- and 5-person suites

Special Features: University-affiliated, privately-owned and operated, Pool, two laundry rooms, recreation room with pool tables, Ping-Pong, and a large screen TV, scheduled housekeeping services, and permit parking

Campus Apartments:

El Dorado Apartment

Contract: 9-month contract

Price: 1 bedroom (2 occupants) $554/month, 2 bedroom (4 occupants) $420/month

Location: 6667 El Colegio Road at the intersection of Los Carneros Road

Total Occupancy: 27 one-bedroom and 23 two-bedroom apartments, all doubles

Special Features: Furnished rooms, pool, on-site laundry facilities, utilities (gas, electricity, water, and garbage pick up) are included, parking is available, but limited, for both undergraduate and graduate students

Santa Ynez Apartments

Contract: 9-month contract for undergrads, 12 month contract for grad students

Price: 2 bedroom (4 undergrads) $420/month, 2 bedroom (2 grads) $734/month

Location: 6750 El Colegio Road (cross street of Los Carneros Road)

Total Occupancy: 200 two-bedroom apartments (150 for undergraduates, 50 for graduates)

(Santa Ynez Apartments continued)

Special Features: Furnished rooms, fitness center, on-site laundry facilities, water and garbage pick up; undergraduate apartments house four residents, graduate apartments house two residents

Westgate Apartments

Contract: 9-month contract

Price: 1 bedroom (2 people) $544/month, studio (1 person) $957/month

Location: 6543 El Colegio Road, adjacent to the west entrance of the UCSB campus

Total Occupancy: 22 studios (singles) and 18 one-bedroom apartments (two people per apartment)

Special Features: For both undergraduate and graduate students, pool, on-site laundry facilities, utilities (electricity, gas, water and garbage pick up) included

Bed Type
Twin (extra-long upon request) or bunk beds

Available for Rent
Microwaves and refrigerators

Cleaning Service?
Yes, every other week in-room, daily in public areas

What You Get
Each student receives a bed, desk, dresser, chair, and Ethernet, cable, and phone hookup options. All dorms have study lounges, quiet hours, computer labs, and theme floors. Some have kitchen-access.

Did You Know?

Interest floors include Substance-Free, Quiet, Rainbow House, Outdoor Adventure, Wellness, Transfer-Living, Global Living Experience, Black/African American Studies, Multicultural Experience, Performing and Creative Arts, Scholars Floor, Chicano/Latino Cultural Studies, Asian/Pacific Islander Cultural Studies, and Women in Science and Technology.

Students Speak Out On...
On-Campus Housing

"I lived on campus, and I would definitely advise it! It's really convenient for your first year and a good way to meet a lot of people."

Q "Dorms are great. **There are off-campus dorms in Isla Vista, as well as the on-campus dorms; both are great**. It doesn't really matter which, but I think it would be better to be on campus."

Q "**Tropicana and Fontainebleu are cool** because they have apartment-like setups that are incredibly fun. On-campus places are very crowded but close to school."

Q "On-campus dorms are okay. The rooms are kind of small. **Most rooms are doubles, but due to overpopulation, some are triples**. On campus, you might have to only share a room with one other person, but you will have a common bathroom with toilets and showers that you share with about 50 people. Off campus, you have Tropicana Gardens, Fontainebleu, and Francisco Torres. Tropicana and Fontainebleu are about the same, but Tropicana is bigger. Fontainebleu is adjacent to campus, and Tropicana is two blocks further. They both have suite-style arrangements—a couple bedrooms to one bathroom—like an apartment. Francisco Torres is the nicest and most expensive. It is also the furthest from campus—about 15 minutes on a bike."

52 | CAMPUS HOUSING   www.collegeprowler.com

Q "**The off-campus dorms are by far better**, but that's where I lived, so I'm biased. I lived in Francisco Torres, which is the farthest from campus, but the most fun. The on-campus dorms are alright, but the rooms are small and often rooms meant to be doubles are made into triples. Some of them even have ocean views. Anacapa and San Nicolas are both pretty good on-campus dorms."

Q "The dorms are alright. **I lived in Francisco Torres, which is kind of far from campus**, at the other end of Isla Vista. It's big, the rooms are pretty nice, and it has the best food of any of the dorms. The Manzanita Village is great! It's right on the ocean and is state-of-the-art."

Q "As far as dorms go, the on-campus ones are the only way to go. **Off-campus ones are ghetto**, and the on-campus ones are between campus and the ocean."

Q "The **dorms on campus are situated in a very nice area**, right by the beach and lagoon."

Q "On-campus dorms are good because you can wake up two minutes before class, whereas if you live in Francisco Torres (FT), you have to make a 10-minute bike ride to class. But I still loved living in FT because the rooms are bigger, I only shared a bathroom with three other people, and there are so many freshmen living there it didn't feel like I was missing out on anything. **FT is a freshman experience all on its own**."

Q "**Try to get on-campus dorms so you can be involved with other new students** and on-campus activities. Some dorms are smaller than others, and the Santa Cruz ones are really nice. I lived in Francisco Torres when it was not owned by UCSB. It was nice, but not very close to campus or well-organized with the on-campus activities. However, that all changed when it became affiliated with UCSB."

Q "Francisco Torres has the best deal. Don't be swayed by its distance from campus—you'll get a good workout from the bike ride. Because everyone lives somewhat farther away than the other freshmen, **everyone living in Francisco Torres has the opportunity to bond**. The rooms are spacious, and each one has a sink in it. Plus, only four people to a suite have to share one bathroom."

The College Prowler Take On...
On-Campus Housing

No matter which dorm you get, it's hard not to have fun when you are suddenly living with 50 other 18-year-old freshmen who just moved out of their parents' house. The only dorm I would steer clear of as a freshman is San Rafael—it has more upperclassmen. Usually, these students have already made all of their friends and are no longer going through the same transitions that freshmen are.

UCSB dorms are either on campus or in Isla Vista. You can put yourself in a lottery for the on-campus dorms, but there's no guarantee that you will be placed there. The on-campus dorms are more crowded, but they're closer to classes and University activities, and some have ocean views. Manzanita Village is the newest and, therefore, still the nicest on-campus dorm. The off-campus dorms have larger rooms and more of an apartment-like feel. Many students like the spacious rooms and the food at Francisco Torres, despite its distance from campus. Each of the dorms have their positives and negatives, and most students are happy with the trade-offs and comfortable with whichever dorm they end up in.

B

The College Prowler® Grade on

Campus Housing: B

A high Campus Housing grade indicates that dorms are clean, well-maintained and spacious. Other determining factors include variety of dorms, proximity to classes and social atmosphere.

Off-Campus Housing

The Lowdown On...
Off-Campus Housing

Undergrads in Off-Campus Housing:

71%

Average Rent For:

Studio Apt.: $900/month
1BR Apt.: $1,000/month
2BR Apt.: $1,800/month

Popular Areas:

Downtown

Goleta

Isla Vista

For Assistance Contact:

The Community Housing Office, (805) 893-4371, located in the University Center, Room 3151 on campus. Their services include off-campus online rental listings, a survival guide, roommate listings, landlord/tenant dispute resolution, roommate dispute resolution, and move-in and move-out videotaping.

Did You Know?

The best time to **start searching for your apartment is in January**, in order to beat the rush of students who will soon be looking for a new place to live. By March, you should sign your lease; you'll be ready to move in to your new home by June or July.

Students Speak Out On...
Off-Campus Housing

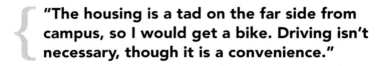

"The housing is a tad on the far side from campus, so I would get a bike. Driving isn't necessary, though it is a convenience."

Q "**Most off-campus housing is literally right next to the ocean**. You will be living blocks or even only houses away from your friends. You'll be a five-minute bike ride to class, and have plenty of food places to hang out, eat, drink a beer, and sit in the sunshine. Isla Vista is probably one of the best college towns in the country."

Q "You have to start apartment-hunting early to get a good place. **It's expensive around here, because the demand far outpaces supply**. You have to look hard; there are some really gross places, and some really nice ones, too. It will take some effort, but you can always find a place. There are resources available through UCSB, and they have workshops to help freshmen when the time comes."

Q "**Housing is very close to campus and right along the beach**. Everyone rides bikes to class, and for the next four years, all of your friends and all of the parties are going to be within walking distance."

Q "If you live off campus, you will be living in Isla Vista, which is basically attached to the campus. It's mostly all college students from UCSB and Santa Barbara City College. **It's a really fun place to live, because it's so close to campus**, you can just walk or ride your bike to school. Everywhere you look, there are people your age."

Q "Isla Vista is where everyone lives off campus. It's normally not that hard to find a place, and **everything is within a five- to ten-minute bike ride**. Unfortunately, because students live in the same places year after year, they get pretty run-down. Needless to say, with all those kids living in such close proximity to each other, things can get out of hand."

Q "It's **not hard to get housing in Isla Vista**, but if you want a cool place, you have to be persistent."

Q "Off-campus housing is pretty convenient; **everything is right off campus and within walking distance**. It's really expensive to live off campus. I live in a two-bed, two-bath apartment that is very run-down and costs almost $2000 a month. Most of the apartments are really expensive and dirty, so watch out. I would suggest living on Del Playa—this street is the biggest party street, but has the nicest houses because it is right on the cliff above the ocean. They are sweet!"

Q "Well, it's expensive and very overcrowded, but a lot of fun. **Don't expect to have your own room because it's just too expensive here.** You have to see it for yourself to really understand, but Isla Vista is right next to the school and houses something like 8,000 students in one square mile. So parking sucks, but it is doable, and everything is crowded, but it's also tons of fun. You're always surrounded by lots of people and things."

Q "I have two comments about renting: **it's easier to get a place if you are a girl**, and definitely try to get your own room, but expect to pay a lot for it."

Q "**It's a lot less expensive to live in a sorority house than to rent from a rental company in Isla Vista.** The sorority houses are clean and you get all of your meals cooked for you in some of the houses. I felt safe because there was an alarm system, a door code, and a house mom."

Q "I had much **more luck renting from private landlords** who just owned one or two properties, than the bigger rental companies who owned half the houses in Isla Vista—they love the fact that there's no rent control. My places were cheaper because the private landlords didn't raise rent by a huge amount every year."

Q "I definitely recommend living in Isla Vista for a few years, even though it can get pricey and some places are run-down. You **definitely have to look early and find a group of people to sign leases with**. Living downtown can also be fun, and since the bus system is efficient, it's also convenient, depending on your schedule."

Q "Isla Vista is an ideal place for students to live. Compared to other campuses that I have visited, the way Isla Vista is set up is really unique and special. **It's very cool that all of your friends live really close**, and that you can run into so many people you know as you bike or walk around. Just stopping by a friend's place or meeting for dinner is so easy in this community."

The College Prowler Take On...
Off-Campus Housing

After awhile, one room for all of your belongings gets old. Venturing out into the town of Isla Vista to rent a house can be quite intimidating, so here is a cheat sheet to guide you through the process of finding a house in Isla Vista:

1. Start looking in January, and try to sign a lease by March. Pick some friends and just walk up to houses you like, knock on the door, and ask if the house is available to rent for the upcoming year.

2. Some houses will have applications available right away, while some are in a lottery.

3. Go to the rental companies like Sierra, BDC, and Ron Wolfe (if you have to) and get their rental lists in order to apply for the houses they own. The Housing Department in the UCen has a good list of "who not to rent from."

4. If you are late in doing all of the above, turn to the *Daily Nexus* and answer some ads. Sometimes housing cooperatives, such as an all-vegetarian house or an athletic team house, are a good way to meet people like you, and to find a place to live.

5. Get used to expensive rents, but if you start early enough, you can find some deals. Houses on Del Playa, although pricey, have great balconies and decks that sit on a cliff overlooking the ocean. Most people say it was worth living on Del Playa for a year, just to experience it.

Goleta and downtown are also good areas to rent in. Goleta is mostly residential neighborhoods, a short drive from campus, and fairly quiet—reminicent of the neighborhoods some students may have grown up in. Rent can be cheaper in Goleta, as well. Downtown is as expensive as Isla Vista. Many students live downtown during their senior year, once they are over the Isla Vista party scene and old enough to go to the downtown bars. Lots of jobs and internships are located downtown, but it's a 15-minute drive to campus. Overall, Santa Barbara has enough housing options that students will most likely find the type of arrangement that best suits their interests—it's only paying for that "perfect place" that can be the problem.

The College Prowler® Grade on

Off-Campus Housing: C-

A high grade in Off-Campus Housing indicates that apartments are of high quality, close to campus, affordable, and easy to secure.

Diversity

The Lowdown On...
Diversity

Native American:
1%

White:
62%

Asian American:
16%

International:
1%

African American:
3%

Out-of-State:
5%

Hispanic:
17%

Political Activity

Overall, students tend to be liberal—this is a California college campus, after all. The student Republican, Democrat, Liberal, and Green groups are vocal and very active on campus. In the past, peace marches and walkouts have taken place. Local politics are also hot topics for UCSB students.

Gay Pride

About 10-15 percent of students identify themselves as gay, lesbian, or bisexual. Although the scene is not big on campus, tolerance is.

Minority Services

- The African American & American Indian Cultural Center (AAAICC) shows cultural films and holds gatherings, art exhibits, receptions, lectures, retreats and community-based presentations on the development of cultural leadership.
- The Asian Resource Center encourages interaction among the different Asian American ethnic groups.
- The MultiCultural Center hosts performances, lectures, film viewings, art exhibits, and other social events for all of the different minority clubs.
- The Disabled Students Program provides readers, note takers, interpreters, referrals, registration assistance, and supplemental orientation.
- The multicultural sororities and fraternities are frequently recruiting at the Arbor on campus.
- The Resource Center for Sexual and Gender Diveristy (RCSGD) is for and about, lesbian, gay, bisexual, transgender, intersex, and allies at UCSB.
- The University Religious Center is for campus ministries of various faiths.
- The Women's Center offers workshops, films, and lectures that explore both the concerns and achievements of women, and houses the Rape Prevention Education Program.

Minority Clubs

Africa Awareness Student Organization, Akanke, American Indian Intern Association, Amitié, Armenian Student Organization, Asian Pacific Student Union, Asian Unity Leadership Committee, Black Pioneer Renaisance Organization, Black Reign, Black Student Union, Cambodian Student Union, Carribe, Chaldo Assyrian Student Alliance, Chicano Latino Cultural Services, Chinese American Association, Chinese Lion Dance Team, Chinese Student Union, Destino, Hail To The Piece (Open Door Prod), Hellenic Club at UCSB, Hermanas Unidas/Unidos de UCSB, Hip Hop Club at UCSB, Hong Kong Student Union, Hui O Lokahi, Iaora'na Te Otea, India Association, Indus, Interethnic Relations In Sisterhood, Iranian Student Group, JEWLS - Jewish Ladies Society, Joining All Cultures Together, Kapatirang Pilipino, Korean Students Association, Lusophone and Hispanic Literature Conference, Merhaba Folkdance Club, Middle Eastern Cultural Club, MUJER, Multicultural Action Coalition, Multicultural Drama Company, Muslim Student Association, Native American Indian Language Study Group, Nikkei Student Union, Queer People of Color, Vietnamese Student Association

Academic/Professional Minority Clubs

AIESEC (an international business organization), Black Pre-Health, Latino Business Association, Los Curanderos (a pre-med organization), Los Ingenieros (an engineering organization), National Society of Black Engineers, Student Chapter of the American Indian Science & Engineering Society

Note: Since campus organizations are registering and re-registering with the University every day, this list is only a sampling of UCSB's current clubs for minority groups. For up-to-the-minute information, check out *www.sa.ucsb.edu/orgs/* where you can sort through UCSB clubs by catagory.

Most Popular Religions

Christianity, Judaism, Catholicism are the top three religions that students identify with on campus.

Students Speak Out On...
Diversity

> **"The campus is fairly diverse; every conceivable group is represented. This is a pretty liberal school, so there isn't much prejudice at all."**

Q "UCSB is not very diverse. **It's a white majority**. The publicity and general knowledge of multicultural events is not very good either, but that's always changeable."

Q "Honestly, our campus is mostly caucasian. There are lots of other groups represented, but it really isn't that diverse. **It's kind of like a bubble**."

Q "This school is not very diverse at all. **It's definitely a predominantly white school**."

Q "As for the demographics, it's not the most ethnically diverse school, that's for sure. I'm Asian and I grew up in the Bay Area, which is by San Francisco. I grew up in a place where Asians made up about 40-50 percent of the population, so going to Santa Barbara was definitely a culture shock for me. It's not like I didn't have white friends in high school, but it just seemed like everyone at UCSB was blond with blue eyes. Once you get past that initial reaction, you find that **people are pretty diverse here—if not culturally, then socially**. You have your business-minded people, your hippies, your stoners, your skaters, and your surfers. All in all, it takes awhile to adjust—at least it did for me—but you come to appreciate it."

Q "It's **not very diverse** here, but diversity is one of the University's goals. They seem to be constantly working towards that."

Q "The UC system tried using affirmative action for a couple years, but has since dropped it. So, **diversity is a problem**. The great majority of students here are white. There are campus organizations and programs for different ethnicities and religions, however."

Q "The **gay community is pretty active on campus**, and is pretty well-tolerated."

Q "If there is **one thing this campus lacks**, it's diversity."

Q "UCSB is the most predominantly-white UC of them all. **Most UCs seem to be Asian-dominated**. There are more and more groups filtering in, though."

Q "Even though Santa Barbara **does not have a very diverse population**, there are many groups and on-school activities that give minority students places to be comfortable and to express themselves."

Q "The campus is fairly diverse; every conceivable group is represented. This is a pretty liberal school, so **there isn't much prejudice at all**."

Q "UCSB is **not racially diverse**, but it does have a lot of diverse personalities that, for the most part, get along together."

Q "My culture shock was mostly due to the huge amount of very rich people both attending UCSB and living in Santa Barbara. Also, I think over **95 percent of the students are from California**, so if you are an out-of-state student, you'll be a minority in that way, for sure."

The College Prowler Take On...
Diversity

Demographically, the UCSB student population is predominantly Caucasian and middle- to upper- class. Diversity on campus, as far as clubs and organizations, is definitely present, although not highly publicized. In other words, the ethnic organizations are important to those who are in them, but invisible to practically everyone else. The University does offer many clubs and services that students can take advantage of, and cultural events are becoming much more popular.

Most students feel comfortable and safe in this community; in fact, although UCSB has the least amount of diversity compared to the other UC campuses, students agree that it probably has the most racial integration. Friends' groups are likely to be racially diverse. Over half of the student body is white, and about a third is split equally between Asian and Hispanic students. The African American student body is small, comprising only three percent of the total population. Students agree that, while not very diverse, the campus does make students of every ethnicity feel welcome, and that tolerance for the gay and lesbian scene is high.

The College Prowler® Grade on

Diversity: C+

A high grade in Diversity indicates that ethnic minorities and international students have a notable presence on campus, and that students of different economic backgrounds, religious beliefs, and sexual preferences are well-represented.

Guys & Girls

The Lowdown On...
Guys & Girls

Women Undergrads:
55%

Men Undergrads:
45%

Birth Control Available?
Yes, at student health you can get a full exam, receive a prescription, and stock up on as many free condoms as you can carry.

Social Scene
Socially, UCSB students excel. Overall, people want to meet each other. Don't be surprised if you get invited to a keg party or an outdoor concert as you walk down the street. In fact, just walk into any big, open house party—you will most likely be welcomed and handed a cup.

Percentage of Students With an Eating Disorder
23.4% of women and 7.9% of men

Hookups or Relationships?
Hookups. Some schools have high marriage rates right out of college and it seems like everyone is settling down and planning futures together. This isn't that school.

Best Place to Meet Guys/Girls
For a hookup, go to an Isla Vista party; for a relationship, meet them at work or through a team.

Dress Code
During the day, guys wear skater or surfer brand names, board shorts, or random thrift store-looking t-shirts. They pretty much wear the same stuff at night, too. Frat boys throw on a collared shirt to go out. Girls mostly wear tank tops year round, and they definitely dress up to go to bars or fraternity houses but stay a bit more casual for parties in Isla Vista. Designer names are definitely a part of many girls' wardrobes. For the most part, everyone seems hygienic. There are a lot of hippies, but everyone seems to have that laid-back, beachy look around here.

Did You Know?

Top Places to Find Hotties:
1. Del Playa Drive, anytime
2. Sands Beach on a hot, weekend day
3. Downtown on a Thursday night

Top Places to Hook Up:
1. The beach
2. In your room (hopefully a single)
3. On a Del Playa balcony
4. Downtown bar
5. Bill's Bus

Students Speak Out On...
Guys & Girls

"Girls and guys are both very attractive on a general basis. You just have to find the ones that are cool."

Q "Well, like most places, **guys around here are drunk and horny on the weekends**! You have to watch yourself, but that's like any other college-party environment. Girls tend to dress pretty skimpy. This is a pretty health-conscious school—meaning a lot of people work out, so there are a lot of good-looking people to been seen and enjoyed."

Q "**Guys are freaking hot here**. It's like going to school with Ken and Barbie sometimes, but beware— some of them aren't too nice, but they are nice to look at, for sure."

Q "There are definitely a lot of good-looking people at this school. Most of them are really down-to-earth and mellow. The vast majority of people are very easy-going, friendly types who are mostly sunbathing beach-goers. I would say **our campus has a lot of good-looking girls and guys**. There's not a lot of ethnicity, but it's all good."

Q "I don't know about guys, but **the women, my god, they are beautiful**. But after a while, your standards start to increase because you've adjusted, so it kind of backfires. At home, girls that used to be hot just don't do it for me anymore."

Q "**There are beautiful people everywhere**—it's Santa Barbara. Of course, there's a wide variety of people, but I have to say that there are some pretty hot girls. The guys are hot, too."

Q "The guys on campus are mostly surfers and skaters. They are pretty much all in good shape because lots of them surf, and the chicks, well, there are plenty of really hot chicks. The guys are cool; they are trying to get laid big time, so know that. But what guys aren't? I've heard that the girls can be kind of stuck-up, but I don't know about that. They all seem pretty cool and nobody really has any problems. **There are tons of people with money, so that might come into play**."

Q "There's a lot of eye candy on both sides, but **there are also a lot of body image and eating disorders**. Also, a lot of people are really into the 'hooking up' scene rather than dating or relationships, so be prepared. Oh yeah, the STD rate is kind of high, so be sure to learn about that."

Q "The guys here are definitely hot, but honestly, they're jerks. The single mentality is pretty much the one that dominates here. **Guys here make great friends but awful boyfriends**."

Q "There are **hot honeys everywhere**!"

Q "There are **definitely a lot of good-looking people at this school**. Most of them are really down-to-earth and mellow."

Q "There are definitely beautiful people of both sexes on the UCSB campus. The **guys are hot, but many of them are slimy and immature**, so watch out! It's an intimidating group to be a part of. You definitely need to be self-confident around here."

Q "The **best way to find a potential relationship is at work or through a campus club**, not at a frat party or at a Del Playa party, where everyone is drunk and is never going to remember your name."

Q "If you come to UCSB with a long-distance relationship, don't hole yourself away in your dorm room on the phone. Make sure that you go out and make friends— **don't isolate yourself, because you will regret not forming friendships your first year**."

Q "The only problem with attractive people everywhere is that **a lot of people are full of themselves, and therefore not very fun to be with**. And I wonder how many of these attractive people are actually hurting themselves to be that way."

The College Prowler Take On...
Guys & Girls

It's hard to beat a surfer boy biking to the beach with his wet suit down to his waist and a surfboard under his arm, or a couple of bikini-clad girls playing volleyball on the sand. Students agree that the hottie level is high here, but they disagree on the inside beauty. Promiscuous and snobby are the negative words associated with some students, but then some described people as extremely friendly and mellow. According to other UCSB students, most don't expect any big dates—UCSB is more of a "spend money on a party that will draw a lot of girls" than a "spend money on one girl" kind of school. Dating occurs, but just not as often as meeting up with your crush at a party or downtown at the bars. Long-term relationships are more likely to be formed through working together at University activities. At least one thing is certain: UCSB students do find each other very attractive. Just about everyone plays some sort of intramural sport, and it's easy to spend most of your time outdoors, which is how a lot of people stay tan and in-shape. Eating disorders, however, apparently run rampant at this campus, probably because everyone is tan and in shape.

The College Prowler® Grade on
Guys: A

A high grade for Guys indicates that the male population on campus is attractive, smart, friendly, and engaging, and that the school has a decent ratio of guys to girls.

The College Prowler® Grade on
Girls: A

A high grade for Girls not only implies that the women on campus are attractive, smart, friendly, and engaging, but also that there is a fair ratio of girls to guys.

Athletics

The Lowdown On...
Athletics

Athletic Division:
Division I

Conference:
Big West

School Mascot:
Gaucho (an Argentinian
cowboy)

School Colors:
Blue and Gold

**Males Playing
Varsity Sports:**
239 (3%)

**Females Playing
Varsity Sports:**
210 (1%)

Men's Varsity Sports:

Baseball

Basketball

Cross-Country

Football

Golf

Soccer

Swimming & Diving

Tennis

Track & Field (outdoor)

Volleyball

Water Polo

Women's Varsity Sports:

Basketball

Cross-Country

Soccer

Softball

Swimming & Diving

Tennis

Track & Field (outdoor)

Volleyball

Water Polo

Club Sports:

Cycling

Field Hockey

Gymnastics

Lacrosse

Rowing

Rugby

Sailing

Snowboarding & Skiing

Surfing

Triathalon

Ultimate Frisbee

Intramurals:

Badminton

Basketball

Bowling

Flag Football

Golf

Racquetball

Running

Sand Volleyball

Indoor and Outdoor Soccer

Softball

Tennis

Ultimate Frisbee

Volleyball

Water Polo

Did You Know?

All sports have both novice and advanced teams. Also, adventure programs include sports such as **rock climbing, backpacking, scuba diving, ropes course, and kayaking**. You can also take physical activities classes that include sailing, bowling, weight lifting, and wine tasting.

Athletic Fields

Campus Diamond (softball), Campus Pool (swimming, diving, and water polo), Caesar Uyesaka Stadium (baseball), Harder Stadium (soccer), the Robertson Gym (men's volleyball), the Thunderdome (basketball, women's volleyball)

Getting Tickets

Free, but don't forget your student ID.

Most Popular Sports

Basketball and volleyball

Best Place to Take a Walk

Out to Campus Point or up the beach to the Butterfly Sanctuary

Overlooked Teams

The surfing team has won six national championships and the ultimate Frisbee team, the rowing team, and the ski/snowboard team have all competed and placed in national championships.

Gyms/Facilities

Intercollegiate Athletics Building

The ICA building is reserved mostly for varsity and club sport use, as well as some athletic classes.

Robertson Gym

Rob Gym houses a gym and gymnastics equiptment and is used for team and club practices and tournaments.

Recreation Center

The Recreation Center, available to any UCSB student, has two pools, several gyms, three weight rooms, a climbing wall, tennis and squash courts, a roller hockey floor, and a Jacuzzi.

Students Speak Out On...
Athletics

> "As for sports, I run cross-country and track, and it has been a big part of my college experience, but UCSB is not a 'jock' school like UCLA. There are plenty of intramural (IM) options."

Q "**Basketball and volleyball are the biggest sports here**. The IM program here is huge. You can play just about any IM sport that you want."

Q "Sports aren't huge on campus. Our basketball teams were decent last year, and normally we do well in volleyball. The **baseball and softball teams are not bad** either. IMs are pretty good; they offer tons of sports, schedules, and leagues."

Q "**Basketball is the biggest varsity sport on campus**; we're a rowdy crowd and well-known for it. IM sports are pretty popular, and there's a wide variety; you can always spot a group of people playing something."

Q "Sports are not a big deal at our school. **We're Division I, and no one seems to care**. It just doesn't get much hype. Intramural sports are cool, though. I played basketball, softball, and roller hockey IMs. You just have to have the initiative to join a team or start one up."

Q "Honestly, I am not really into the sports scene on campus; they are kind of weak. **IM sports are a lot of fun**, though. I was involved in them and really enjoyed it."

Q "There isn't as much school spirit as there is at UCLA sporting events. **Varsity sports aren't huge events that everyone goes to**, but they are fun events when you do go. The IM program is great and has anything you want to play. Lots of fun."

Q "The recreational-sports department is wonderful! There are many club sport teams to choose from which all require no previous experience and are highly competitive. There is also a variety of IM sports to choose from, each with varying competitiveness. You can put the group together yourself and play with all your friends. You can always find activities and sports to join at UCSB. The varsity sports (I am referring to intercollegiate sports, but should be more specific because many of the club sports teams are competitive on a varsity level) also do well each year. **The swim team and the women's volleyball team have been doing well for a long time**."

Q "Storming the court when the **men's basketball team won the Big West tournament a couple years ago** was one of the highlights of my college career."

Q "Varsity sports, unfortunately, are only big to those who play them. **Club sports are a way to go if you are looking to be competitive** or try something new. I recommend heading over to the Rec Cen with your dorm floor and getting the lowdown on the intramural options."

Q "Our sports teams are good, but **you don't hear a lot about them**."

The College Prowler Take On...
Athletics

Some of the varsity sports teams at UCSB are actually very good, frequently winning their divisions and making it to national tournaments, yet it seems like half of the school is oblivious. Basketball and volleyball games can usually draw large and loud crowds, but without a football team, UCSB lacks the media spotlight and big campus athletes that other campuses draw. Still, club sports are highly competitive and well-organized.

Surfing, ultimate Frisbee, rowing, sailing, and snowboarding and skiing have had exceptional seasons in the past. Although most students can't claim to have watched many games, practically everyone can say that they have participated in an intramural sport through the Recreation Center. Intramurals are divided into laid-back, just-for-fun teams and I-was-the-star-in-high-school teams. A lot of people have made great friends, relieved stress, and had a lot of fun in the IM program. It's difficult to grade the athletics at UCSB because while the intramural and club sports are fantastic, the varsity sports are seemingly non-existent at times. UCSB does not have the typical football Saturdays and high-energy athletic team spirit that many other larger universities have. But if you actually want to participate in athletics and get out there and play, this is a great place to be.

The College Prowler® Grade on

Athletics: B

A high grade in Athletics indicates that students have school spirit, that sports programs are respected, that games are well-attended, and that intramurals are a prominent part of student life.

Nightlife

The Lowdown On...
Nightlife

Club and Bar Prowler:
Popular Nightlife Spots!

Isla Vista:
Dublin's Sports Grill
910 Embarcadero del Norte
(805) 685-1503

Hailed as the best college bar around, Dublin's attracts a crowd who wants to watch the game on the big screen TV, sing karaoke, play pool and air hockey, or just hang out for awhile.

The Study Hall
6543 Pardall Rd.
(805) 685-0929

The Study Hall has a full bar and gets packed with students who don't want to make the drive downtown. Frequently it is a big Greek place. The Study Hall is the most popular bar in Isla Vista. Happy hour Monday–Friday 4–7 p.m.

→

Downtown:

James Joyce

513 State St.

(805) 962-2688

A great, chill bar on State St. Sometimes they have live music, sometimes the pool table is open, but they always have lots of free peanuts!

Madison's Sports Grill

525 State St.

(805) 882-1182

As another student favorite, Madison's has a nice patio on State St., so you can wave to friends and people-watch while you drink. After the games, the bar transforms into a crowded dance floor, providing jello shot specials and some well drink specials.

Q's Sushi A Go Go

409 State St.

(805) 966-9177

Q's is three floors, each with a bar on it. The first floor has a dance floor, an outside patio, and a sushi bar (during dinner hours). The third floor has about eight pool tables. Many stop by for the all-you-can-eat sushi buffet and a few drinks to kick off their evenings.

Sharkeez

416 State St.

(805) 963-9680

Sharkeez is one of the most popular downtown bars, especially on Thursday nights. Sharkeez also has decent happy hour deals, a full menu, TVs, and a dance floor. It's laid-back during the day, but definitely a drink-hard, dance-hard bar at night.

Zelo

630 State St.

(805) 966-5792

Both a nightclub and a restaurant, Zelo offers jazz music during dinner, and local DJs and bands after 10 p.m.

Other Places to Check Out:

Hades is the gay bar in town. The Press Room, Elsie's, and Dargan's are more local, sit-at-the-bar places downtown, a little off of State Street. Also try Wildcat Lounge, Joe's Cafe, Santa Barbara Brewing Co., Velvet Jones, The Brewhouse, The Blue Agave, Absinthe, Jimmy's Oriental Garden, the Sportsman, Calypso Bar and Grill, and Indochine

Favorite Drinking Games:

"The Loop," which is having one beer at every establishment in Isla Vista that serves alcohol (don't forget the Laundry Lounge).

(Favorite Drinking Games, continued)

Century Club

Quarters

Edward Forty-Hands (Duct tape two 40s to your hands. You can't do anything until you finish both.)

Kings

Student Favorites:

Sharkeez, Q's, Madison's

Bars Close At:

Midnight in Isla Vista, 2 a.m. downtown

Primary Areas with Nightlife:

Isla Vista house parties, Isla Vista bars on Pardall Street, and downtown bars.

Local Specialties

There is Santa Barbara Blonde beer at Santa Barbara Brewing Company. You can also order a "Santa Barbara Sunset" at Longboard's or Enterprise Fish Co. Or, just get a Sex on the Beach shot—not really a Santa Barbara invention, but it could have been.

Organization Parties

Global Studies parties, Geography hikes, Ski and Snowboard Club parties, surf team parties

Frats

See the Greek section!

What to Do if You're Not 21

Alex's Cantina for dancing

Del Playa/Isla Vista parties

The Living Room and the Coach House are 18 and over and frequently host bands.

Real Life (Thursday nights on-campus) or Reality (Friday nights downtown) are hosted by the college Christian groups, and Hillel Jewish Center dinners/parties occur weekly

Zelo, for college nights, with a cover

Zodo's Bowling & Beyond

Useful Resources for Nightlife

Bill's Bus is a service that takes Isla Vista residents to and from the bars downtown. It runs Tuesday through Saturday nights. A round-trip ticket is about $6—much less expensive than the $25 cab ride.

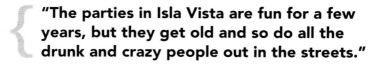

Students Speak Out On...
Nightlife

"The parties in Isla Vista are fun for a few years, but they get old and so do all the drunk and crazy people out in the streets."

Q "Downtown is a good alternative for nightlife and can be really fun. **Most of the bars on State Street are great**. Madison's and Sharkeez are two of my favorites."

Q "**The Study Hall is the best local bar—it's so much fun to go there for a casual drink**. There are tons of bars and clubs in downtown Santa Barbara, but I only really go there on weekend nights because you have to take the bus. There's not a very big club scene here. I'm from Vegas, so everything is pretty mellow to me."

Q "**The bars and clubs downtown are pretty cool**. I just turned 21, and I'm having a blast! There's this thing called Bill's Bus that takes you downtown and back for something like six dollars. It's really fun because everyone's on it and having a great time."

Q "The only real bar in Isla Vista is the Study Hall; it's a great place to chill. There are also a lot of smaller places that serve beer. **If you like dancing, you need to go downtown to State Street**. On certain nights, Zelo is an 18-and-over club, but it sucks. Q's, and Madison's are all pretty good clubs. The James Joyce is a great bar downtown."

Q "UCSB gets an unfair rap for being a party school, but **it's just as much a party school as any other campus**. The difference is that the community is so compact that all the parties are centrally located on the same street, making it really easy to have a good time."

Q "It's not as great as you would expect. On weekends, you get a lot of the mid-life crisis crowd trying to blend, and music is too trendy. **On weeknights, it can be fun because that's when college nights happen**, but not everyone always wants to go out on Thursday nights—at least the people who care about school and have strong willpower don't."

Q "Pretty much **every Friday and Saturday night, you can walk along the street and just go into random parties**. As for the bars and clubs, they are also situated on State Street. It's all within three blocks, so when you get tired of one bar, you can walk on to the next one. It's pretty cool. My favorite one is Q's; it's three levels. The first one is the bar and dance floor, the second is like a catwalk where you can sit or stand and watch people downstairs dancing, and the third floor has pool tables and another bar. It's my favorite bar, hands down. My next favorite is Madison's, which is about a block down from Q's. Madison's has TVs right in front of the urinals, so you can watch SportsCenter while relieving yourself, which is pretty nifty."

Q "There's a great party scene downtown and in Isla Vista. Basically, you don't need clubs freshman year; **Del Playa is a street in Isla Vista that will suit all your party needs**. There are free parties at beachfront homes and there's always a good time to be had, depending on what you think is fun—sometimes it can get a little out of hand."

Q "There's a great bar scene downtown. I only turned 21 during the spring of my senior year, so I didn't get to go out too much, but it's a lot of fun. There's only one bar in Isla Vista. People go downtown for the bars, but there are **parties almost every weekend in Isla Vista,** at the fraternities, or on Del Playa—that's what most people do."

Q "Del Playa is right on the ocean, just a few blocks off campus, where parties will rage during the early part and the end of the quarters. **Thousands of kids walk the streets, and there's music blasting from balconies and lights flashing all over the place**; it's way fun. There are parties every weekend and during the week, too."

Q "The parties range from a couple of close friends playing drinking games or watching a movie, to parties with hundreds of people that walk in off the street because you have a band playing in your front yard, and more kegs than you remember bringing in the backyard. Downtown **bars are the same way; they range from dance halls to quieter pool halls**."

The College Prowler Take On...
Nightlife

One of the best things about UCSB is that you don't have to be 21 to experience some sort of nightlife. House parties occur every weekend in Isla Vista. The first weekend of the school year, you will have to hold hands with your friends in order to stay together in the crowds of partiers out on the streets. You will undoubtedly be able to frequent many, many college keg parties throughout your time here. And, just as you tire of the Isla Vista party scene, you turn 21 and get to experience the downtown bar scene! Although not comparable to big-city clubs, the bars downtown are fun and have some variety, from loud places with blaring dance music to mellow hangouts where guests can lounge. Santa Barbara is the place out-of-towners come to party. Just a warning: it's very difficult to use a fake ID at the bars in Santa Barbara and police will regularly do ID checks. Besides, there is plenty of fun to be had in Isla Vista, so waiting out 21st birthdays isn't too hard.

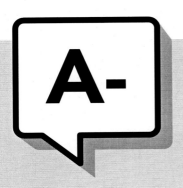

The College Prowler® Grade on

Nightlife: A-

A high grade in Nightlife indicates that there are many bars and clubs in the area that are easily accessible and affordable. Other determining factors include the number of options for the under-21 crowd and the prevalence of house parties.

Greek Life

The Lowdown On...
Greek Life

Number of Fraternities:
11

Number of Sororities:
11

Undergrad Men in Fraternities:
10%

Undergrad Women in Sororities:
12%

www.collegeprowler.com

Fraternities on Campus:

Alpha Epsilon Pi

Alpha Gamma Omega

Alpha Tau Omega

Beta Theta Pi

Phi Sigma Kappa

Pi Kappa Alpha

Sigma Chi

Sigma Nu

Sigma Phi Epsilon

Sororities on Campus:

Alpha Chi Omega

Alpha Delta Pi

Alpha Epsilon Phi

Alpha Phi

Delta Delta Delta

(Sororities, continued)

Delta Gamma

Gamma Phi Beta

Kappa Alpha Theta

Kappa Kappa Gamma

Pi Beta Phi

Other Greek Organizations:

Greek Council

Greek Peer Advisors

Interfraternity Council

Order of Omega

Panhellenic Council

Multicultural Colonies

8 sororities: Alpha Kappa Alpha (historically African American), Chi Delta Theta (Asian American interest), Delta Sigma Theta (historically African American), Lambda Sigma Gamma (multicultural), Lambda Theta Nu (Latina/Chicana interest), Sigma Alpha Zeta (multicultural), Sigma Kappa Chi (Asian American interest), Zeta Phi Beta (historically African American)

7 fraternities: Alpha Phi Alpha (historically African American), Gamma Zeta Alpha (Latin interest), Kappa Alpha Psi (historically African American), Lambda Phi Epsilon (Asian American interest), Nu Alpha Kappa (Chicano interest), Sigma Chi Omega (multicultural), Zeta Phi Rho (multicultural)

> "Greek life doesn't dominate. Everyone can have fun, especially if you're a girl. All frat parties are pretty much open to girls, and Del Playa always has parties to go to."

Q "I'm anti-Greek, but that's just me. Unlike UCLA or a lot of other schools here, Greek life is totally optional. **We have a lot of parties that are not Greek-sponsored**. You don't have to be in the Greek system."

Q "**Greek life at UCSB is definitely in the minority**, but it's still very strong. You do not need to be Greek to have fun here, but being Greek definitely adds to the excitement and options of things to do."

Q "The Greek system is okay, but it hasn't taken over the social scene. From what I hear about my friends who visit from other campuses, **our Greek system is very strong, and our parties are hot**."

Q "The Greek life is cool. I'm in a sorority and I enjoy it; however, it's not the only thing going on socially. Actually, **it is easier to party when you aren't in one** because of all the rules they have established on campus."

Q "I'm a Greek, and honestly, **Greek life is not all there is to do on campus**. Don't get me wrong; I love being in a house, but it's not necessary if you want to have fun."

Q "Greek life is present, but **not many people participate**."

Q "**Greek parties are great because anyone can walk into a frat or sorority party**, but it's mostly Caucasian Greek life that gets the hype. The ethnic Greeks do put on parties, but you usually have to find out beforehand. After freshman year, though, you learn that the beer runs out quickly, and guys have trouble getting in."

Q "Personally, **I hate the Greek system**. The thing about UCSB is that you don't need to be in a frat or sorority to party. If you want to party, you just go down to Del Playa."

Q "Actually, Greek life isn't a large component of the student body or the social scene, but Greek life does make itself known. I was in a fraternity, and I enjoyed it very much. Anyway, **if you go Greek, you'll have a ton of fun; if you don't go Greek, you will also have fun.**"

Q "Greek life is big, but it does not dominate. If you're into that scene, I would suggest joining. Some of my friends are in fraternities and they love it—**a 24/7 party is what it's about**. They all have houses off campus; they're pretty nice, big places with plenty of parties."

Q "There's a fairly big Greek system, but it definitely doesn't overwhelm. If you're into that, you have lots of choices, but **if you're not into it, you won't feel left out**."

Q "The Greek life is here, but it does not take over the social scene at all. **People don't really have a need for it**. There are tons of house parties here with free beer and stuff, so the Greek scene is small, but existent."

Q "Greek life exists, but **you can avoid it** (as I would recommend) and still have a social life."

Q "Greek life in Santa Barbara is considerably laid-back, but it is thriving. If you find the right house for you, it can be a really incredible experience. **My advice is to not write it off completely without checking it out**. I met so many people rushing, and half of them never joined a house but still made friends and had a fun week. If you do join a house, make an effort to have friends outside the system, too. Overall, why not give it a chance and see if you like it?"

The College Prowler Take On...
Greek Life

Less than 15 percent of UCSB students choose to go Greek. Because Santa Barbara is full of so many other ways to have a social life and to make friends, fewer people turn to the Greek system. Even though the percentage of UCSB students who are Greek is small, they definitely have a voice and a presence in Isla Vista, and on campus. The Greek system has undergone a lot of changes in its bureaucracy and its conduct rules to the point that, as organizations, they are held to stricter conduct rules than the rest of UCSB students. Still, it's another opportunity you can take advantage of, and can be a great part of your college experience. Rush is also a good way to transition into college and to meet lots of people right away as a freshman. UCSB's sororities do not haze and have a rush program that is less strenuous than other universities with very high Greek percentages. At the same time, students can make lots of friends and have social opportunities without going Greek.

The College Prowler® Grade on

Greek Life: B-

A high grade in Greek Life indicates that sororities and fraternities are not only present, but also active on campus. Other determining factors include the variety of houses available and the respect the Greek community receives from the rest of the campus.

Drug Scene

The Lowdown On...
Drug Scene

Most Prevalent Drugs on Campus:
Marijuana
Alcohol

Liquor-Related Referrals:
616

Liquor-Related Arrests:
56

Drug-Related Referrals:
102

Drug-Related Arrests:
43

Drug Counseling Programs:
Student Health Services
Alcohol/Drug
Awareness Program

Students Speak Out On...
Drug Scene

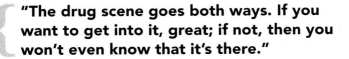

{ **"The drug scene goes both ways. If you want to get into it, great; if not, then you won't even know that it's there."**

Q "Drugs are available if you want them. I am not into the drug scene, but I have friends who have done anything from pot to ecstasy to cocaine. **If you want it, you can find it**."

Q "**The most revalent drugs are pretty much just alcohol and some marijuana**. The Greek system tends to have some harder stuff."

Q "Personally, I am not into drugs at all, but **there is definitely a cocaine scene**, and there are, of course, people who smoke weed. It's not overwhelming; if you're into that sort of thing you can find it, and if not, it's easy to avoid."

Q "You'll find anything you look for; all you have to do is ask. Weed is very popular and abundant. I have seen people do coke, and I've heard of people doing 'E.' I just drink. **Also, be very careful about the date rape drugs**. At a party, never take a drink from someone you don't know. A lot of people smoke pot, and to a lesser extent there are pockets of other drugs. It's by no means pervasive, and it's very easy to avoid if you want to."

Q "There's a lot of weed, and other hard drugs around, but I think that goes for any college campus. **Everyone's tried something at least once**."

Q "As for drugs, if you like them, then UCSB is the place to be. In Santa Barbara, it just seems a lot more convenient. For instance, in my household alone, there were four dealers. And on my street, there were at least six or seven other houses you could've gone to. If you want ecstasy, crack, or anything at all, I can't imagine it to be too hard to find. With that said, **there were a couple of drug busts in my neighborhood**."

Q "If you want them, they're easy to find. If you don't want them, it's no problem. **I've never felt real pressure to take drugs**, which has a lot to do with who you decide to hang out with. If you're hanging out with the right kind of people, whatever that means to you, then there's no problem."

Q "If you want it, then most likely there's a way to get it without too much effort. **It's college-what do you expect**? I'm not too much into the scene."

Q "I don't do drugs, so **I never really saw them**. If that's the way you want to be, then you won't really see it, either. But there is pot and other drugs. It's out there if you want it."

Q "**You're cool if you do and cool if you don't**—as long as you find the right people to hang with."

Q "There is **a problem with drinking and drugs** in Isla Vista."

Q "This is a party school. **Count on drugs being around**."

Q "I don't even think of pot as a drug anymore. Every job I have had here, **my co-workers and employees smoke. Half of my friends' parents smoke**. Seriously, I forget that it isn't legal."

The College Prowler Take On...
Drug Scene

Drinking and smoking pot are a big part of the culture here; however, many students choose not to partake and get through four years without feeling any pressure. A documentary was filmed at UCSB asking people on campus how long it would take them to "hook up a gram" and the average answer was 10 minutes. Obviously, drugs are definitely available. Cocaine, ecstasy, and mushrooms are the other drugs that frequent Isla Vista, but students say that they don't see these harder drugs if they're not looking for them. For the most part, students do not overly abuse drugs to the point that they fail out of classes and don't graduate. It really is up to you whether you participate in the drug scene or not, and this level of participation translates into what drugs you will and won't see on campus. If you're looking, you'll probably find a variety of illegal substances. If not, then it's likely that you won't see too much drug use, especially with the harder ones.

The College Prowler® Grade on

Drug Scene: C+

A high grade in the Drug Scene indicates that drugs are not a noticeable part of campus life; drug use is not visible, and no pressure to use them seems to exist.

Campus Strictness

The Lowdown On...
Campus Strictness

What Are You Most Likely to Get Caught Doing on Campus?

- Drinking
- Stealing a bike

Students Speak Out On...
Campus Strictness

{ **"The drinking policy is pretty strict on campus, but we used to drink in the dorms all the time and never got caught."**

 "It's not the campus police you worry about when partying—nine times out of ten you will be off campus in Isla Vista or around Del Playa. There you will face the IV Foot Patrol. The Foot Patrol walks up and down DP and through IV looking for kids who are making idiots out of themselves, puking, making a scene, or urinating in public. As long as you're cool and don't attract attention, you're gold. On campus, **they say no drinking in dorms, blah, blah . . . just keep it quiet**, and you won't have to worry about it. It goes on, and they know it; just don't make a scene."

Q "I got caught cheating on my take-home final and ended up getting a B in the class—I don't plan on cheating ever again because it was stressful thinking about what could have happened to me, but I do think that the **school's threats on suspending or expelling students for cheating and plagiarizing is kind of a joke**."

Q "They're strict; if you walk around outside with a cup, it must be turned upside down. There is also a **parental notification program** in case you get into trouble."

Q "It's **easier to party when you aren't in a dorm** because of all the rules they have established."

Q "**You can get away with a lot in Isla Vista**. The basic rule is that if you're using common sense, you'll be fine. They won't come into a party to break it up unless it's causing a huge disturbance or if they see trouble brewing."

Q "On campus, you get expelled from the dorms for drugs, but there's an initial warning for alcohol. I'd say it's what you would expect. However, **there isn't any penalty for coming home drunk and high**."

Q "The main things people get arrested for or cited for in Isla Vista on a Friday night is public intoxication, possession, and peeing where you're not supposed to. **If you're walking on Del Playa, just make sure you have your cup upside down**, and don't go peeing in the bushes or else the cops will catch you. There was a time when some friends of ours went into our carport area in the back and urinated; the cops caught them and gave them $135 tickets."

Q "The **campus is not that strict on drinking or drugs**. Most people drink a whole lot, so you will be around that often. Basically, just watch out for yourself and there shouldn't be any problems."

Q "**As long as you don't do anything really stupid, you'll be fine**. I'm not sure what the policies are exactly, but where you really need to worry is in Isla Vista because they have their own deputies and they commonly arrest people or give them citations for being drunk in public, biking or driving under the influence, minors in possession of drugs or alcohol, and urinating in public."

Q "Well, the campus police aren't the ones you really have to watch out for. The **Isla Vista Foot Patrol roams around at night during the party scene and are incredibly strict** about people walking around with alcohol and walking around drunk. But it really isn't a big deal; you just have to know how to handle yourself, and then you're fine."

Q "Umm, **it's all pretty relaxed**. You can get away with a lot, within reason."

Q "On campus, the police have it under control. In Isla Vista, the police manage to take care of the scary stuff and let the fun stuff happen for the most part. But on nights that are notoriously big party nights, **I have seen police lining the streets and setting up barricades**."

The College Prowler Take On...
Campus Strictness

Campus strictness varies a bit since the campus police are entirely different from the Isla Vista Foot Patrol. The campus police patrol campus, but students who aren't out-of-control or having really loud parties don't have to worry about them too much. Off campus, the Isla Vista Foot Patrol allows big parties, but as soon as it hits midnight and they see kegs in plain view, or a foot hits the sidewalk when you are holding an open container, they become very strict. IVFP are also known for writing tickets for biking under the influence, being a minor in possession, being drunk in public. The University notifies parents of tickets students recieve by sending them a copy in the mail.

As far as cheating and plagiarism, some professors are extremely adamant about checking essays and creating multiple copies of tests. Definitely do not attempt to cheat or plagiarize because you will most likely get caught, and depending on your professor, you could face major repercussions. If you take care of yourself and stay in control, you'll be absolutely fine and never have a run-in with the Foot Patrol or the Campus Conduct Boards.

B

The College Prowler® Grade on

Campus Strictness: B

A high Campus Strictness grade implies an overall lenient atmosphere; police and RAs are fairly tolerant, and the administration's rules are flexible.

Parking

The Lowdown On...
Parking

Approximate Parking Permit Cost:
$324–432 yearly, $113 quarterly, $36 monthly, and $8 daily

UCSB Parking Services:
(805) 893-2346
www.tps.ucsb.edu

Freshmen Allowed to Park?
Yes

Common Parking Tickets:
Expired Meter: $40
No Parking Pass: $40
Expired Day Pass: $40
(If you get a ticket, you can pay or contest it online at: *www.scapay.com*, or go to the Parking Services building behind the softball field.)

Student Parking Lot?
Yes

Parking Permits

As long as you live more than two miles away from campus, you can purchase a parking permit. Freshmen who live on campus can buy a year parking permit, although it may be a long walk from their dorm to their parking space—it's determined through a lottery. Three-hour and daily passes are sold everyday and night to those who would like to park on campus but do not have a permit.

Did You Know?

Best Places to Find a Parking Spot
By the Humanities and Social Sciences Building (HSSB) or in the Mesa Parking Structure

Good Luck Getting a Parking Spot Here!
Near the library or by Campbell Hall

Students Speak Out On...
Parking

> **"Parking isn't really an issue because, most likely, you will be living in Isla Vista—it's basically attached to campus."**

Q "Parking is a nightmare. On campus or in Isla Vista, **you will spend some time looking for spots, so try not to move your car when you get one**. If you live on campus, you can get your own spot by your dorm for that year. And if you live off campus, apartment complexes usually have a spot for you to share with roommates. You won't have to drive to school, though, unless you live downtown, or in Goleta. Living in IV or on campus, riding a bike or skateboard is key."

Q "**Parking on campus sucks**. Don't have a car if you are a freshman—you don't need it, and it's not worth it. I have been here for three years without a car. You can always take the bus."

Q "Parking sucks because **there are no spots**, plus if you live closer than two miles to campus, you can't get a parking permit. You have to ride your bike."

Q "**Parking is pretty lame**. Even if you buy a year-long pass for campus, it doesn't guarantee that you'll get a spot anywhere close to where you need to be. Isla Vista parking is also pretty bad."

Q "Your first year of parking will be in remote lots around campus. **There really is no driving and parking when you go to your classes**; it's either walking or biking. Walks are not long, and biking is even easier than that."

Q "It's not easy to park and it's expensive, so **get a bike, a ride, take the bus, or walk**. The administration keeps taking parking away from students and giving it to staff and faculty, so it takes longer to find a parking spot than it does to just walk to school. Parking off campus is almost impossible as well, so that option isn't very good either."

Q "**Parking is a big negative**. I don't know how it is on campus, but, in Isla Vista, depending on where you live, it can be tough to find a spot on the street. The closer you are to the beach, the harder it is. Del Playa is the worse street to find parking. When I lived on DP, there were times where I would have to park a block over and three blocks back. You don't really need a car, though. It definitely comes in handy, but you can get around campus and IV with just a bike. It's only when you want to go downtown or into Goleta that a car would be needed."

Q "You can get parking if you live in the dorms, but **it's kind of out of the way**."

Q "Parking sucks, but generally, **people don't drive to campus here; we bike**. Everything is really close, so it's not that big of a deal."

Q "Parking sucks. **It's expensive**. I suggest a boycott."

Q "**As long as you have a parking permit, parking on campus is easy** enough, except on rainy days when everyone is really lazy and willing to buy a day pass for $8."

The College Prowler Take On...
Parking

"Sucks" and "lame" are the two most often-used words when it comes to parking on campus and in Isla Vista.

The campus itself has enough spaces to accommodate all of the cars, but that does not mean that students will find a space anywhere close to where they are headed. A day pass is $8, and a year pass is either $324 or $432, depending on the area, but students can only buy one if they can prove that they are a "commuter" who lives more than two miles away from campus. Overall, parking is a nightmare—and even more so in Isla Vista. Isla Vista has no guarantees on parking. Soon, though, UCSB students become the world's best parallel parkers, managing to squeeze cars into spaces they would never have attempted before. If students don't get a reserved parking space that comes with their house or apartment, they usually plan on spending at least five to ten minutes driving around in search of a spot and do not naively assume that the police are going to let anything slide when it comes to tickets. Now, it's probably starting to make a little more sense why everyone is in love with his or her bike around here.

The College Prowler® Grade on

Parking: D+

A high grade in this section indicates that parking is both available and affordable, and that parking enforcement isn't overly severe.

Transportation

The Lowdown On...
Transportation

Ways to Get Around Town:

On Campus

Ride a bike—you will blend in with the 14,000 others on the bike paths that take you everywhere you would need to go. The roundabouts take some practice—stick to the outside of the bike loops.

Walk or use a CSO Escort if it's late: (805) 893-2000

Use a UCSB shuttle if you have a disability.

Public Transportation

MTD Bus, free with your student ID. Schedules are on all the buses. They don't run very late at night, so be sure to plan ahead.

Taxi Cabs

Absolute Cab:
(805) 898-1669

Beachside Taxi:
(805) 966-5600

California Cab:
(805) 568-5105

Economy Cab:
(805) 964-9800

➡

(Taxi Cabs, continued)

Fiesta Taxi:
(805) 564-4000

The Yellow Cab Co.:
(805) 965-5111

Car Rentals

Alamo
local: (805) 967-1202
national: (800) 327-9633
www.alamo.com

Avis
local: (805) 965-1079
national: (800) 831-2847
www.avis.com

Budget
local: (800) 964-6791
national: (800) 527-0700
www.budget.com

Enterprise
local: (805) 966-3097
national: (800) 736-8222
www.enterprise.com

Hertz
local: (805) 967-9489
national: (800) 654-3131
www.hertz.com

National
local: (805) 967-1202
national: (800) 227-7368
www.nationalcar.com

Best Ways to Get Around Town

Chip in for gas and borrow your friend's car

Bike

Take the bus

Start walkin' . . . use the beach as your reference point, and you can find practically everything. However, you should know that the coast curves, so sometimes the ocean is south and sometimes it is west.

Ways to Get Out of Town:

Airlines Serving Santa Barbara

Alaska Airlines
(800) 252-7522
www.alaskaair.com

American Eagle/Airlines
(800) 433-7300
www.aa.com

America West
(800) 327-7810
www.americawest.com

Northwest
(800) 225-2525
www.nwa.com

Airport

Santa Barbara Airport

It can sometimes be considerably less expensive to fly out of LAX or Burbank airport. You can take the Santa Barbara Airbus shuttle (about $68 roundtrip, (805) 964-7757) to LAX.

How to Get to the Airport

Take the "airport" exit from the 217 Freeway.

A cab ride to the Airport costs $20, but only because it is a flat rate. The airport is actually next to campus. Convince your roommate to drive you.

Greyhound

34 W. Carrillo St.
local: (805) 965-7551
national: (800) 231-2222

Amtrak

209 State St.
local: (805) 963-1015
national: (800) 872-7245

Travel Agents

STA Travel, located in the University Center (UCEN)

Holman Travel:
(805) 564-6764

Santa Barbara Travel Bureau:
(805) 966-3116

Students Speak Out On...
Transportation

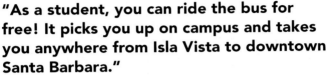

"As a student, you can ride the bus for free! It picks you up on campus and takes you anywhere from Isla Vista to downtown Santa Barbara."

Q "The bus system is alright. I used it a lot during my freshman year when I lived at the dorms. **Just make sure you get on the right bus.** One time, I got on the wrong one or it changed numbers right when I got on; my friend and I had to sit through a two-hour bus ride all over downtown."

Q "The **public transportation is convenient**. The city bus is free to UCSB students and runs seven days a week."

Q "**The bus system is pretty convenient**. I don't use it very often, although I have a car and ride my bike to campus."

Q "There are buses that can **get you pretty much anywhere**."

Q "You can get a bike here at a used bike auction for really cheap. **Bikes are a way of life here**."

Q "Don't have a car if you are a freshman—you don't need it, and it's not worth it. I have been here for three years without a car. **You can always take the bus**."

Q "Bikes and buses can get you pretty much anywhere. The only time I really didn't like not having a car was grocery shopping. **Taking groceries back on the bus, or on a bike, is not fun**, but usually a friend is willing to help out with that sort of thing."

The College Prowler Take On...
Transportation

You can survive without a car at UCSB; in fact, most students prefer to not have to deal with the horrible parking scene. Bikes are the most popular form of personal transportation, and students say that you can get just about anywhere on the bus. With that said, having a car, especially if you live off campus, is incredibly convenient. If you get a job, want to go grocery shopping, catch a movie, or just want to get out of the dorms for the weekend, it's much easier to use your car instead of planning a bus route. The buses do not run so often that you can just go to a random bus stop and wait a couple of minutes. You have to plan out your day ahead of time to coincide with the bus if you want to go anywhere outside of Isla Vista or campus. The bus system is reliable, clean, and free, so no one can complain too much, but as a backup plan, you might want to be really nice to the suitemate who brought a car to school. And, bring a bike if you can—but don't forget a bike lock.

B-

The College Prowler® Grade on

Transportation: B-

A high grade for Transportation indicates that campus buses, public buses, cabs and rental cars are readily available and affordable. Other determining factors include proximity to an airport and the necessity of transportation.

Weather

The Lowdown On...
Weather

Average Temperature:

Fall:	72 °F
Winter:	58 °F
Spring:	65 °F
Summer:	72 °F

Average Precipitation:

Fall:	.50 in.
Winter:	.20 in.
Spring:	1.6 in.
Summer:	.02 in.

Students Speak Out On...
Weather

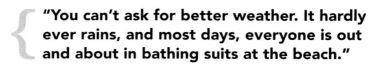

"You can't ask for better weather. It hardly ever rains, and most days, everyone is out and about in bathing suits at the beach."

Q "**UCSB is literally on the beach**. If you like sunshine, ocean breezes, and a general temperature in the high 60s to mid 70s . . . you'll love it here. We get some rain in the winter quarter and a little fog now and then, but it's beautiful here. I surf; I love it."

Q "Most of the time, the weather here is pretty good. It can get cloudy in the morning, but it burns off. **We live in one of the most beautiful places in the world**, I think."

Q "The **weather here is amazing**! You cannot ask for better weather. It's beautiful all year-round. If you love the beach, this is the place for you."

Q "The weather is absolutely beautiful here, right on the beach. **It is usually about 70 degrees and rarely rains**. We have a little rainy season during winter quarter, but this year it was really nothing."

Q "The weather is awesome. **Fall and spring are great**. Winter varies—sometimes it's really warm, but other years it will rain for a month straight. Summers are awesome, too."

Q "**It's not too cold and not too hot**. It doesn't rain much and isn't too humid in the summers."

Q "Most of the time, the weather is great. **It's very mild; not too hot and not too cold**. It can be overcast at times, but it's basically California weather."

Q "Gorgeous! The sunsets are like no other. **There's sun, ocean, and a cool breeze**—wonderful. Of course, there's always a little rainy season, but it's no big deal. In fact, it's sometimes even fun."

Q "The **weather's mostly beautiful and sunny**, but we're right on the ocean, so it gets cold and windy at night. Winters are usually only different because of the rain."

Q "**Imagine beach weather, and you have Santa Barbara**. It's nothing to complain about."

Q "Most people feel that the weather here is amazing. It's sunny 90 percent of the year, with a few days of rain in the fall and winter. **Temperatures vary only slightly and usually stay between 70 and 90 degrees**. The breeze off of the ocean keeps the temperatures from getting too high."

Q "The weather really **doesn't get any better**."

Q "The weather is beautiful; it's California. **We have about one to two months of wet weather in the winter**, and the rest of the time it's sunny and mild. It's never as hot as it gets in LA during the summer."

Q "The weather has been getting warmer every year. There is a little cold and a little rain, and **be prepared for fog most mornings**."

Q "For California, Santa Barbara can get 'cold' at night and during the winter months. But **you never have to change out of your wardrobe**; flip-flops, jeans, and tank-tops work all year."

The College Prowler Take On...
Weather

Beautiful sunsets and sunrises, ocean breezes, clear skies, and temperatures mostly in the 70s are a college student's dream. But those at UCSB don't have to dream. Santa Barbara, California has fantastic weather, especially compared to the weather horror stories from most other college towns. Although Santa Barbara sounds deceptively sunny year-round, it can occasionally rain and get foggy and cold. The name for June is "June Gloom" in Santa Barbara because the marine layer in the summer usually hangs out over the coast until the sun burns it off sometime after lunch. These are minor complaints, however, about infrequent deviations from a near-perfect climate. Overall, Santa Barbara is seasonless—you can wear jeans and a T-shirt almost everyday of the year and girls wear tank tops to go out to parties throughout the year (whether it's cold or not). Just don't make the mistake of only packing tank tops and swimsuits—you will be buying a sweatshirt the first week of school for that one day a week it gets cloudy.

The College Prowler® Grade on

Weather: A+

A high Weather grade designates that temperatures are mild and rarely reach extremes, that the campus tends to be sunny rather than rainy, and that weather is fairly consistent rather than unpredictable.

Report Card Summary

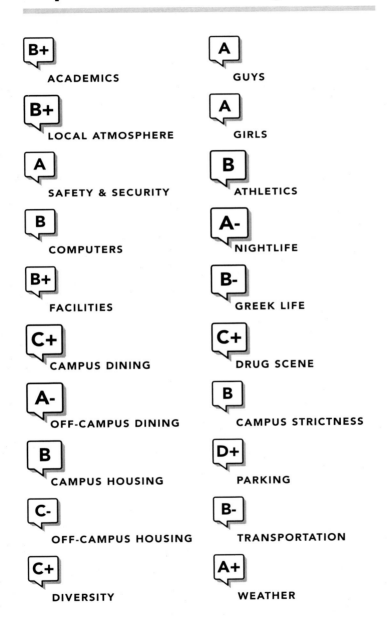

B+ ACADEMICS

B+ LOCAL ATMOSPHERE

A SAFETY & SECURITY

B COMPUTERS

B+ FACILITIES

C+ CAMPUS DINING

A- OFF-CAMPUS DINING

B CAMPUS HOUSING

C- OFF-CAMPUS HOUSING

C+ DIVERSITY

A GUYS

A GIRLS

B ATHLETICS

A- NIGHTLIFE

B- GREEK LIFE

C+ DRUG SCENE

B CAMPUS STRICTNESS

D+ PARKING

B- TRANSPORTATION

A+ WEATHER

Overall Experience

Students Speak Out On...
Overall Experience

"I love this school. It definitely has its positives and negatives, like anywhere, but I can honestly say that I am very happy to be here."

Q "I have been to a lot of colleges visiting friends, and to tell you the truth, I am stoked to be here. The people are nice, the weather is great, the surf is a little inconsistent, but you can't have it all, right? **I'm going to miss this place when I'm done** because it's a lot of fun and a great place to be."

Q "Overall, my campus experience at UCSB has been awesome. I love it here. **Coming to UCSB is the best thing that's ever happened in my life**. It's very fun, and I'm happy with my choice."

Q "I do wish I was somewhere else just because I've lived in the city all my life, and the people here are just too different from what I'm used to. Also, **the counseling staff is horrible; they're not very courteous**. Frankly, I don't think they like their jobs because everyone I talk to in a couple of different departments always has some sort of complaint."

Q "I love this place. **The people, the scenery, the partying, and the academics are all great**. I wouldn't want to be anywhere else right now."

Q "I wouldn't change my experience here for anything in the world. **I love UCSB** so much!"

Q "All-in-all, **UCSB was a great experience**. I don't think I will ever be in that type of situation again with that lifestyle and that kind of environment. It's something I regret not taking advantage of more. Honestly, my first two years there, I didn't really like it that much. But, after you get used to it and appreciate it for what it is, then it's a really cool place."

Q "Freshman year was a blast. I did at one point have the feeling I didn't fit in and felt that this school lacked something I wanted. But, now I love it here, and I'm glad I chose this school. It's got character. **It's a party school, so be prepared for that, but it's also rising in academic standing** and improving every day."

Q "My overall experience is that I loved the time I spent here, and wish I could stay more than four years. **I'd say about 30 percent of the students do stay for five years because they love the lifestyle so much**. If you party and are laid-back, you will enjoy it. I think that studying here is fun and not very hard, but we are known for our party-school image, so keep that in mind; we definitely live up to this."

Q "Ironically, UCSB was not my first choice at all, and I didn't really even want to go here at first. Now that I'm here, **it's great, and I can't picture myself anywhere else**. I have honestly learned so much and don't regret any part about being here."

Q "I can't tell you how much this school has changed my life. **I have been here for three years, and I wish I could stay for four or five more**. The school's location is second to none. I mean, what other school teaches surfing for a Phys Ed class? The people are unbelievably chill and warm-hearted. I came here not knowing a soul, and after my first year, I knew so many unique individuals. I guess you could say that I love my school all around."

Q "**UCSB has some of the worst undergraduates around**. But there are those that try hard and subsequently do well. Unfortunately, this is a 'party school,' and it lives up to its reputation. If you're serious about your classes, you can get a great education here and work with some fantastic professors."

Q "My overall college experience has been unbelievable. **I cannot see myself anywhere else**. The location, the education—everything has been great."

Q "I wouldn't change my experience here for anything in the world. **I love it so much**!"

Q "I absolutely love UCSB. **Who couldn't love a school with oceanfront property** to take your morning jog on? There's a niche here for everyone."

Q "I personally love it here and so do about 98 percent of my friends. **The people are great, the area is great, and the school is beautiful**."

Q "I took five and a half years to graduate—not because I got involved with too much partying and slacking, but because **I got involved in all of the extra activities** that the University had to offer, such as sports, studying abroad, a multiple-subject major, Greek life, campus jobs, and volunteer opportunities."

Q "I had a very difficult decision to make when I was choosing my college. I narrowed it down to UCSB and an Ivy. **I chose UCSB and haven't regretted it once**. This campus and city have everything to offer, from academic challenges to sports to volunteer work—if you are pro-active about what you want to do, you can find it here."

Q "I couldn't be happier with my decision to attend UCSB. **The past four years have been the best in my life**."

The College Prowler Take On...
Overall Experience

UCSB students can't say enough good things about this place—most never want to leave. Whether it's the academics, the weather, the social scene, or the laid-back atmosphere, practically all students fall in love with something here. And, if you do get the urge to leave, LA is an hour and a half south, the wine country is half an hour inland, San Francisco is five hours north, and San Diego is four hours south. You can spend your entire four years exploring Isla Vista and Santa Barbara, as well. Tourists pay money to get to hang out here for a vacation, and we get to live here, full-time! Give yourself a chance to get to know the school and the town. It can take a year to find your type of friends or your major or your favorite club, but if you are actively searching, you will be able to find what you are looking for at UCSB. The students who excel at UCSB are independent and able to take care of themselves. Students have to be able to resist the social temptations a party school presents and plan their own schedules, while still keeping their well-being in mind—the school is too big to hold everyone's hand. Overall, UCSB is the true college experience that many high-school students have been anxiously awaiting. Sure, it doesn't have a football team, but who needs that when students can spend Saturdays surfing or playing football game with friends, right on the beach?

The Inside Scoop

The Lowdown On...
The Inside Scoop

UCSB Slang:

Know the slang, know the school. The following is a list of things you really need to know before coming to UCSB. The more of these words you know, the better off you'll be.

ACCESS Card – Your student ID card. You can put money on it and use it as a debit card on campus.

The Alternative – A copy shop in Isla Vista where students will have to buy many readers (see definition).

Arbor – The area outside Girvetz Hall that has coffee, a little convenience store, and food stands.

AS – Associated Students, the student government on-campus.

AS Notes – Class notes (sometimes taken by the teaching assistant) for sale.

BARC – Billing Accounts/Receivable Collections, the cashier's office that takes student tuition checks.

→

CAB – Community Affairs Board, the student-run community service group.

Campus Point – A student publication and the end of campus that juts out into a point with ocean on both sides.

CLAS – Campus Learning Assistance Services, where students drop-in to get help on papers or weekly tutoring for science and math classes.

CSO – Campus Security Officer, a student who will escort other students home, or give you a ticket for biking in a walkway.

Devereux – The beach right below the Del Playa cliffs.

DLG – De La Guerra, a cafeteria on campus.

FT – Francisco Torres dormitory, located off campus at the end of Isla Vista.

Gaucho – The UCSB mascot, an Argentinian cowboy.

GOLD – Gaucho On-Line Data, current student secure site used to sign-up for classes, check grades, request transcripts, etc.

HSSB – The Humanities and Social Sciences Building.

The Hub – The bottom floor of the University Center, which has fast food and sometimes hosts concerts.

IV – Isla Vista, the square-mile town next to UCSB.

IVFP – The Isla Vista Foot Patrol.

KCSB – The student-run radio station located under Storke Tower.

MCC – The MultiCultural Center.

Nexus – The student-run daily newspaper.

Perm Number – Student ID number; located on student ACCESS cards.

RBR – The Reserve Book Room, a part of the library open 24 hours which checks out books/articles that professors has put on reserve.

Reader – A booklet of all the handouts for a class that students buy at one of the copy shops at the beginning of the quarter (professors will specify which copy shop).

SBCC – The Santa Barbara City College.

SAASB – The Student Affairs and Administrative Services Building.

Storke Tower – You'll see it!

Sands – An Isla Vista beach.

Thunderdome –The Events Center.

Trop – Tropicana Gardens, an off-campus dorm with suite-style living.

Things I Wish I Knew Before Coming to UC Santa Barbara

- Each dorm has a computer network, so your files can be shared with everyone else, and vice versa.

- You will be dropped if you miss the first two days of a class.

- You can access the library database from home.

- AS Bike Shop on campus will lend you tools and tell you how to fix your bike for free.

- If you are an undecided major, do not take your General Education requirements as Pass/No Pass because then they cannot count for the major you eventually choose.

- Videotape your apartment before you move in to save yourself from losing your entire security deposit when you move out.

- Dead Week, the period before finals, is actually only one or two days

- Freshman Seminar classes are fun and a great way to make friends.

- Student Health is less expensive than anywhere else in town.

- The beaches have natural tar on them sometimes (use baby oil to remove).

- A quarter is short—it takes awhile to get used to the fact that professors discuss midterms the second week of class.

- Lock your tire to your bike frame and the rack, otherwise you will just have a frame or a tire left.

- Expect to get made fun of as a freshman if you are walking with your entire floor down Del Playa, all wearing black pants—it's just part of being a freshman.

- Easy Mac and microwave popcorn are really good at midnight when the cafeteria is closed.

- If you go to Student Health, they charge your BARC account, so if your parents pay your student bills, plan on them knowing that you went. (Get your STD test at Planned Parenthood if you're paranoid.)

Tips to Succeed at UC Santa Barbara

- Learn how to "crash" a class (which means to add a class that you didn't sign up for ahead of time).
- Don't try to study in your dorm room—go to the library.
- Go to office hours.
- Attempt to understand how to schedule classes—and make sure to find out when your pass time is so you do not miss out on registering as soon as you can. Classes will fill up!

UC Santa Barbara Urban Legends

- Someone jumped off Storke Tower and fell into the Reflection Pool.
- The campus is on Chumash Indian burial grounds.
- Aldous Huxley, who wrote Brave New World, hung out in Isla Vista.
- Francisco Torres was a Holiday Inn before it was a dorm.
- Isla Vista has more bikes than anywhere but China.
- The ocean oil rigs off the coast are really casinos.

School Spirit

UCSB school spirit is pathetic compared to some other big, Division I universities. Most blame the fact that we don't have a football team. But, Gaucho Locos, the student club that attends sporting events in bright yellow shirts, are fun, rowdy and very spirited. You can join for $5, get a T-shirt, and make lots of high-spirited friends!

The Easiest Place to Get a Job

Telemarketing for Bargain Network or the UCSB Annual Fund

On-Campus Jobs at the UCen

The Most Sought-After Jobs

Any serving or bartending job

Internships in entertainment industry

Lifeguarding

Traditions

- Varsity Sport Streaking on Del Playa
- Halloween
- Extravaganza, a yearly outdoor concert
- 4/20 and Earth Day celebration in the park
- Throwing tortillas and wearing leis at graduation
- The Chancellor attends a Del Playa party every year
- Burning couches in Isla Vista
- Completing "The Loop" (drinking a beer at every establishment in Isla Vista) before you graduate
- Getting on the wall at the Study Hall

Finding a Job or Internship

The Lowdown On...
Finding a Job or Internship

Go to the Career Services Web site, which will direct you to *monstertrak.com*. Monstertrak has the most up-to-date and local internships—exactly what you need while you are still in school. The other main way to find out about internship and job opportunities is to sign-up for your department's listserv. A lot of businesses will purposely contact the department that they want applicants to come from.

Advice
Do not be afraid to open the Santa Barbara phone book, find the best local place that does what you want to do, and keep calling them. Businesses around here are used to students coming to them and are open to student employees. Be persistent. Although peer-career counselors can help with some information, try to make an appointment with a professional career counselor that has specific knowledge about your major and/or career field.

Career Center Resources & Services

Go to *www.career.ucsb.edu* to get advice on everything listed below, or stop by and pick up a free career packet with resume/cover letter examples, networking tips, and lots of other tips that you will undoubtedly appreciate at some point. Make an appointment or drop in for these career counseling services:

Career Counseling

Placement Advising

Career Workshops

The Resource Center

Graduate School Advising

www.MonsterTrak.com

Grads Who Enter Job Market Within

1 Year: 82%

Alumni

The Lowdown On...
Alumni

Web Site:
www.ia.ucsb.edu

Office:
UCSB Alumni Association
Santa Barbara, CA 93106
(805) 893-2288

Services Available:
Career Connections, Alumni
Discounts, member rates on
insurance and credit cards

Major Alumni Events:
Alumni Association Golf
Classic Tournament, reunions,
Gaucho Getaway trips,
chapters located across
the U.S.

Alumni Publication:
Coastlines Magazine

Did You Know?

Famous UC Santa Barbara Alums

Bob Ballard – Discovered the Titanic

Benjamin Bratt – Actor

Michael Douglas – Actor

Faisal Fahad – Prince of Saudi Arabia

Jack Johnson – Musician

Giondomenico Picco – Assistant Secretary General to the United Nations

Joe Redfield – Pirates baseball player

Brian Shaw – Celtics and Heat basketball player

Student Organizations

If UCSB doesn't have a club you want to join, you can create your own! Just head down to the Office of Student Life, and fill out the form. You will get free Web hosting and free publicity in the *Nexus* on Mondays. Here's a short list of some UCSB clubs:

Academic Affairs

Academic Bowl Club at UCSB

Accounting Association

ACLU (promotes civil liberties)

Africa Awareness Student Organization

AIESEC (global awareness through student exchange in the business environment)

Aikido Club

American Students for Israel

Amnesty International

Anime Club at UCSB

Armenian Student Organization

Art History Club

Asian Pacific Student Union

Bhakti-Yoga Club

Bhangra Team at UCSB

Black Culture Week

Blood Drive Committee at UCSB

Book Club

Brothas from Otha Mothas
(male acapella ensemble)

Business Economics Association

CALPIRG (environmental and public interest club)

Cambodian Student Union

Campus Democrats at UCSB

Dance Club

Gaucho Locos (promotes Gaucho athletics)

Gaucho Pep Band

Hillel

Hip Hop Club at UCSB

Naked Voices (coed pop/rock acapella group)

Queer Student Union

Reel Loud Exhibitions
(silent films with live performances)

Screenwriters' Co-op

Ski & Snowboard Club

Surfrider Foundation

Swing and Ballroom Dance Club

Taiwanese Student Association

Note:

Since campus organizations are registering and re-registering with the University every day, this list is only a sampling of UCSB's current clubs. For up-to-the-minute information, check out: *www.sa.ucsb.edu/orgs* where you can sort through UCSB clubs by catagory.

The Best & Worst

The Ten **BEST** Things About UC Santa Barbara

1 The laid-back beach atmosphere.

2 Lots of opportunities to get involved in different things.

3 There are concerts at the Santa Barbara Bowl, the Hub on campus, and all of the student bands performing for free in Isla Vista on the weekends.

4 There are lots of good food options.

5 You can ride your bike literally anywhere.

6 The weather: you can almost always go outside and play.

7 You never have homework over winter or spring break, because the quarter ends right before both.

8 The friendly, knowledgeable faculty.

9 Good-looking people that wear swimsuits and tank tops year-round . . . sometimes you feel like you are living at a resort.

10 It's the genuine college experience that most people want and expect.

The Ten WORST Things About UC Santa Barbara:

1 There is no football team.

2 The administrative staff is really impersonal—nobody really makes an effort to help students, and they have to be responsible for double-checking their own credits. It takes a lot of effort to figure out where to go and what to do.

3 You don't finish the school year until mid-June.

4 Isla Vista has bad parking and loud partying.

5 Nobody wants a relationship.

6 There is a high cost of living.

7 The really bad landlords and no rent control in Isla Vista.

8 The streets are frequently dirty and full of trash after weekend nights.

9 Restaurants and movie theatres downtown close too early.

10 Cops are heavy-handed on ticketing.

Visiting

The Lowdown On...
Visiting

Hotel Information:

Closest to UCSB:

Bacara Resort & Spa
8301 Hollister Ave.
(805) 968-0100
Distance from Campus:
7.57 miles
Price Range: $550–$1,050

**Best Western
South Coast Inn**
5620 Calle Real

**(Best Western South Coast
Inn, continued)**
(805) 967-3200
Distance from Campus:
3.72 miles
Price Range: $113–$171

Faculty Club (on campus)
UCSB
(805) 893-3096
Distance from Campus:
0 miles
Price Range: $72–$102

➜

Holiday Inn
5650 Calle Real
(805) 964-6241
Distance from Campus:
3.80 miles
Price Range: $119–$134

Pacifica Suites
5490 Hollister Ave.
(805) 683-6722
Distance from Campus:
2.25 miles
Price Range: $145–$175

Ramada Limited
4770 Calle Real
(805) 964-3511
Distance from Campus:
4.16 miles
Price Range: $110–$240

On State St:

El Prado Inn
1601 State St.
(805) 966-7920
Distance from Campus:
9.71 miles
Price Range: $179–$210

Upham Hotel
1404 De la Vina
(805) 962-0058
Distance from Campus:
9.17 miles
Price Range: $185–$295

On the Beach:

Cabrillo Inn at the Beach
931 E. Cabrillo Blvd.
(800) 648-6708
Distance from Campus:
11.73 miles
Price Range: $79–$159
Ask for the UCSB Discount to
receive 10% off

Fess Parker's DoubleTree Resort
633 E. Cabrillo Blvd.
(805) 564-4333
Distance from Campus:
11.37 miles
Price Range: $285–$895

The Four Seasons Biltmore
1260 Channel Dr.
(805) 969-2261
Distance from Campus:
14.95 miles
Price Range: $520–$820

West Beach Inn
306 W Cabrillo Blvd.
(805) 963-4277
Distance from Campus:
10.40 miles
Price Range: $165–$185

Campus Tours

Monday-Friday at 12 a.m. and 2 p.m. in the Visitor's Center, which is the first floor of the Student Affairs and Administrative Services building (SAASB). The Admissions Presentation starts at 11 a.m. Transfer advising seasons are held on Thursdays and Fridays at 1:00 p.m. Park in the Mesa Parking Structure.

Take a Campus Virtual Tour

Visit *www.admit.ucsb.edu* and click on Virtual Tour and Campus Slideshow.

To Schedule a Group Information Session or Interview

Sign up at *www.admit.ucsb.edu* by clicking on "Visit UCSB" and then "Group Tours," or call (805) 893-4518. You can have a session online or in-person.

Directions to Campus

Driving from the North
- Take US 101 South and exit on Glen Annie/Storke Road.
- Turn right on Storke Road.
- Turn left on El Colegio Road.
- Drive straight through into campus.

or

- Take US 101 South.
- Exit on 217 Freeway/UCSB, and merge to the right.
- The freeway will be a dead-end at campus.

Driving from the South
- Take US 101 North.
- Take the UCSB/217 Freeway exit, and merge to the left.
- The freeway will be a dead-end at campus.

Words to Know

Academic Probation – A suspension imposed on a student if he or she fails to keep up with the school's minimum academic requirements. Those unable to improve their grades after receiving this warning can face dismissal.

Beer Pong/Beirut – A drinking game involving cups of beer arranged in a pyramid shape on each side of a table. The goal is to get a ping pong ball into one of the opponent's cups by throwing the ball or hitting it with a paddle. If the ball lands in a cup, the opponent is required to drink the beer.

Bid – An invitation from a fraternity or sorority to 'pledge' (join) that specific house.

Blue-Light Phone – Brightly-colored phone posts with a blue light bulb on top. These phones exist for security purposes and are located at various outside locations around most campuses. In an emergency, a student can pick up one of these phones (free of charge) to connect with campus police or a security escort.

Campus Police – Police who are specifically assigned to a given institution. Campus police are typically not regular city officers; they are employed by the university in a full-time capacity.

Club Sports – A level of sports that falls somewhere between varsity and intramural. If a student is unable to commit to a varsity team but has a lot of passion for athletics, a club sport could be a better, less intense option. Even less demanding, intramural (IM) sports often involve no traveling and considerably less time.

Cocaine – An illegal drug. Also known as "coke" or "blow," cocaine often resembles a white crystalline or powdery substance. It is highly addictive and dangerous.

Common Application – An application with which students can apply to multiple schools.

Course Registration – The period of official class selection for the upcoming quarter or semester. Prior to registration, it is best to prepare several back-up courses in case a particular class becomes full. If a course is full, students can place themselves on the waitlist, although this still does not guarantee entry.

Division Athletics – Athletic classifications range from Division I to Division III. Division IA is the most competitive, while Division III is considered to be the least competitive.

Dorm – A dorm (or dormitory) is an on-campus housing facility. Dorms can provide a range of options from suite-style rooms to more communal options that include shared bathrooms. Most first-year students live in dorms. Some upperclassmen who wish to stay on campus also choose this option.

Early Action – An application option with which a student can apply to a school and receive an early acceptance response without a binding commitment. This system is becoming less and less available.

Early Decision – An application option that students should use only if they are certain they plan to attend the school in question. If a student applies using the early decision option and is admitted, he or she is required and bound to attend that university. Admission rates are usually higher among students who apply through early decision, as the student is clearly indicating that the school is his or her first choice.

Ecstasy – An illegal drug. Also known as "E" or "X," ecstasy looks like a pill and most resembles an aspirin. Considered a party drug, ecstasy is very dangerous and can be deadly.

Ethernet – An extremely fast Internet connection available in most university-owned residence halls. To use an Ethernet connection properly, a student will need a network card and cable for his or her computer.

Fake ID – A counterfeit identification card that contains false information. Most commonly, students get fake IDs with altered birthdates so that they appear to be older than 21 (and therefore of legal drinking age). Even though it is illegal, many college students have fake IDs in hopes of purchasing alcohol or getting into bars.

Frosh – Slang for "freshman" or "freshmen."

Hazing – Initiation rituals administered by some fraternities or sororities as part of the pledging process. Many universities have outlawed hazing due to its degrading, and sometimes dangerous, nature.

Intramurals (IMs) – A popular, and usually free, sport league in which students create teams and compete against one another. These sports vary in competitiveness and can include a range of activities—everything from billiards to water polo. IM sports are a great way to meet people with similar interests.

Keg – Officially called a half-barrel, a keg contains roughly 200 12-ounce servings of beer.

LSD – An illegal drug, also known as acid, this hallucinogenic drug most commonly resembles a tab of paper.

Marijuana – An illegal drug, also known as weed or pot; along with alcohol, marijuana is one of the most commonly-found drugs on campuses across the country.

Major –The focal point of a student's college studies; a specific topic that is studied for a degree. Examples of majors include physics, English, history, computer science, economics, business, and music. Many students decide on a specific major before arriving on campus, while others are simply "undecided" until declaring a major. Those who are extremely interested in two areas can also choose to double major.

Meal Block – The equivalent of one meal. Students on a meal plan usually receive a fixed number of meals per week. Each meal, or "block," can be redeemed at the school's dining facilities in place of cash. Often, a student's weekly allotment of meal blocks will be forfeited if not used.

Minor – An additional focal point in a student's education. Often serving as a complement or addition to a student's main area of focus, a minor has fewer requirements and prerequisites to fulfill than a major. Minors are not required for graduation from most schools; however some students who want to explore many different interests choose to pursue both a major and a minor.

Mushrooms – An illegal drug. Also known as "'shrooms," this drug resembles regular mushrooms but is extremely hallucinogenic.

Off-Campus Housing – Housing from a particular landlord or rental group that is not affiliated with the university. Depending on the college, off-campus housing can range from extremely popular to non-existent. Students who choose to live off campus are typically given more freedom, but they also have to deal with possible subletting scenarios, furniture, bills, and other issues. In addition to these factors, rental prices and distance often affect a student's decision to move off campus.

Office Hours – Time that teachers set aside for students who have questions about coursework. Office hours are a good forum for students to go over any problems and to show interest in the subject material.

Pledging – The early phase of joining a fraternity or sorority, pledging takes place after a student has gone through rush and received a bid. Pledging usually lasts between one and two semesters. Once the pledging period is complete and a particular student has done everything that is required to become a member, that student is considered a brother or sister. If a fraternity or a sorority would decide to "haze" a group of students, this initiation would take place during the pledging period.

Private Institution – A school that does not use tax revenue to subsidize education costs. Private schools typically cost more than public schools and are usually smaller.

Prof – Slang for "professor."

Public Institution – A school that uses tax revenue to subsidize education costs. Public schools are often a good value for in-state residents and tend to be larger than most private colleges.

Quarter System (or Trimester System) – A type of academic calendar system. In this setup, students take classes for three academic periods. The first quarter usually starts in late September or early October and concludes right before Christmas. The second quarter usually starts around early to mid–January and finishes up around March or April. The last academic quarter, or "third quarter," usually starts in late March or early April and finishes up in late May or Mid-June. The fourth quarter is summer. The major difference between the quarter system and semester system is that students take more, less comprehensive courses under the quarter calendar.

RA (Resident Assistant) – A student leader who is assigned to a particular floor in a dormitory in order to help to the other students who live there. An RA's duties include ensuring student safety and providing assistance wherever possible.

Recitation – An extension of a specific course; a review session. Some classes, particularly large lectures, are supplemented with mandatory recitation sessions that provide a relatively personal class setting.

Rolling Admissions – A form of admissions. Most commonly found at public institutions, schools with this type of policy continue to accept students throughout the year until their class sizes are met. For example, some schools begin accepting students as early as December and will continue to do so until April or May.

Room and Board – This figure is typically the combined cost of a university-owned room and a meal plan.

Room Draw/Housing Lottery – A common way to pick on-campus room assignments for the following year. If a student decides to remain in university-owned housing, he or she is assigned a unique number that, along with seniority, is used to determine his or her housing for the next year.

Rush – The period in which students can meet the brothers and sisters of a particular chapter and find out if a given fraternity

WORDS TO KNOW | 143

or sorority is right for them. Rushing a fraternity or a sorority is not a requirement at any school. The goal of rush is to give students who are serious about pledging a feel for what to expect.

Semester System – The most common type of academic calendar system at college campuses. This setup typically includes two semesters in a given school year. The fall semester starts around the end of August or early September and concludes before winter vacation. The spring semester usually starts in mid-January and ends in late April or May.

Student Center/Rec Center/Student Union – A common area on campus that often contains study areas, recreation facilities, and eateries. This building is often a good place to meet up with fellow students; depending on the school, the student center can have a huge role or a non-existent role in campus life.

Student ID – A university-issued photo ID that serves as a student's key to school-related functions. Some schools require students to show these cards in order to get into dorms, libraries, cafeterias, and other facilities. In addition to storing meal plan information, in some cases, a student ID can actually work as a debit card and allow students to purchase things from bookstores or local shops.

Suite – A type of dorm room. Unlike dorms that feature communal bathrooms shared by the entire floor, suites offer bathrooms shared only among the suite. Suite-style dorm rooms can house anywhere from two to ten students.

TA (Teacher's Assistant) – An undergraduate or grad student who helps in some manner with a specific course. In some cases, a TA will teach a class, assist a professor, grade assignments, or conduct office hours.

Undergraduate – A student in the process of studying for his or her bachelor's degree.

ABOUT THE AUTHOR

Writing this guidebook has been such a fun way to finish off my college experience, and it has been a great outlet for all of my UCSB knowledge. I also appreciate the chance to write about a subject that I truly care about. In four years, I lived in the dorms, rushed a sorority, went on Semester at Sea, managed a business, learned how to sail a little, survived a year living on Del Playa Drive, had more than a few part-time jobs, took a wine class, lived downtown, and spent a year interning at *Santa Barbara Magazine* and the Alumni Association publications. Maybe most importantly, I majored in English and minored in writing and professional editing. The skills I acquired and the voice I discovered through my writing classes at UCSB have prepared me for a future media-writing career.

Thanks to my family—Mom, Dad, and Laura—and to my best college friends, Michelle, Erin, Cara, Jenn, Ryan, Reid, Kari, Mark, Alyssa, Alison, and Nate, who all contributed great advice about UCSB. Thanks to my high-school friends (also a big part of my college experience), Melissa, Whitney, and Vickie. And, of course, thanks to College Prowler for allowing me to compose this guidebook.

Enjoy your college experience as much as I did—I hope this guidebook will help!

Kate Sandoval
katesandoval@collegeprowler.com

Notes

....

....

....

....

....

....

....

....

....

....

....

....

....

Notes

....

....

....

....

....

....

....

....

....

....

....

....

Notes

....

....

....

....

....

....

....

....

....

....

....

....

....

Notes

Notes

....

....

....

....

....

....

....

....

....

....

....

....

....

Notes

Notes

....

....

....

....

....

....

....

....

....

....

....

....

....

Notes

....

....

....

....

....

....

....

....

....

....

....

....

....

....

Notes

....

....

....

....

....

....

....

....

....

....

....

....

....

Notes

....

....

....

....

....

....

....

....

....

....

....

....

....

Notes

Notes

....

....

....

....

....

....

....

....

....

....

....

....

....

Notes

....
....
....
....
....
....
....
....
....
....
....
....
....

Notes

....
....
....
....
....
....
....
....
....
....
....
....
....

Notes

....

....

....

....

....

....

....

....

....

....

....

....

....

Notes

....

....

....

....

....

....

....

....

....

....

....

....

....

Notes

Notes

....

....

....

....

....

....

....

....

....

....

....

....

....

Notes

....

....

....

....

....

....

....

....

....

....

....

....

....

Notes

....

....

....

....

....

....

....

....

....

....

....

....

....

Notes

....

....

....

....

....

....

....

....

....

....

....

....

....

Notes

....

....

....

....

....

....

....

....

....

....

....

....

....

California Colleges

California dreamin'?
This book is a must have for you!

CALIFORNIA COLLEGES
7¼" X 10", 762 Pages Paperback
$29.95 Retail
1-59658-501-3

Stanford, UC Berkeley, Caltech—California is home to some of America's greatest institutes of higher learning. *California Colleges* gives the lowdown on 24 of the best, side by side, in one prodigious volume.

New England Colleges

Looking for peace in the Northeast?
Pick up this regional guide to New England!

NEW ENGLAND COLLEGES
7¼" X 10", 1015 Pages Paperback
$29.95 Retail
1-59658-504-8

New England is the birthplace of many prestigious universities, and with so many to choose from, picking the right school can be a tough decision. With inside information on over 34 competive Northeastern schools, *New England Colleges* provides the same high-quality information prospective students expect from College Prowler in one all-inclusive, easy-to-use reference.

Schools of the South

Headin' down south? This book will help you find your way to the perfect school!

SCHOOLS OF THE SOUTH
7¼" X 10", 773 Pages Paperback
$29.95 Retail
1-59658-503-X

Southern pride is always strong. Whether it's across town or across state, many Southern students are devoted to their home sweet home. *Schools of the South* offers an honest student perspective on 36 universities available south of the Mason-Dixon.

Untangling
the Ivy League

The ultimate book for everything Ivy!

UNTANGLING THE IVY LEAGUE
7¼" X 10", 567 Pages Paperback
$24.95 Retail
1-59658-500-5

Ivy League students, alumni, admissions officers,
and other top insiders get together to tell it like it is.
Untangling the Ivy League covers every aspect—from
admissions and athletics to secret societies and urban
legends—of the nation's eight oldest, wealthiest, and
most competitive colleges and universities.

Need Help Paying For School?
Apply for our scholarship!

College Prowler awards thousands of dollars a year to students who compose the best essays. E-mail scholarship@collegeprowler.com for more information, or call 1-800-290-2682.

Apply now at ***www.collegeprowler.com***

Tell Us What Life Is Really Like at Your School!

Have you ever wanted to let people know what your college is really like? Now's your chance to help millions of high school students choose the right college.

Let your voice be heard.

Check out *www.collegeprowler.com* for more info!

Need More Help?

Do you have more questions about this school? Can't find a certain statistic? College Prowler is here to help. We are the best source of college information out there. We have a network of thousands of students who can get the latest information on any school to you ASAP. E-mail us at info@collegeprowler.com with your college-related questions.

E-Mail Us Your College-Related Questions!

Check out *www.collegeprowler.com* for more details.
1-800-290-2682

Write For Us!
Get published! Voice your opinion.

Writing a College Prowler guidebook is both fun and rewarding; our open-ended format allows your own creativity free reign. Our writers have been featured in national newspapers and have seen their names in bookstores across the country. Now is your chance to break into the publishing industry with one of the country's fastest-growing publishers!

Apply now at ***www.collegeprowler.com***

Contact editor@collegeprowler.com or
call 1-800-290-2682 for more details.

Pros and Cons

Still can't figure out if this is the right school for you?
You've already read through this in-depth guide; why not
list the pros and cons? It will really help with narrowing down
your decision and determining whether or not
this school is right for you.

Pros	Cons
....	....
....	....
....	....
....	....
....	....
....	....
....	....
....	....
....	....
....	....
....	....
....	....
....	....

Pros and Cons

Still can't figure out if this is the right school for you?
You've already read through this in-depth guide; why not
list the pros and cons? It will really help with narrowing down
your decision and determining whether or not
this school is right for you.

Pros	Cons
....	....
....	....
....	....
....	....
....	....
....	....
....	....
....	....
....	....
....	....
....	....
....	....
....	....

Albion College	Franklin & Marshall College	Ohio State University	University of Colorado
Alfred University	Furman University	Ohio University	University of Connecticut
Allegheny College	Geneva College	Ohio Wesleyan University	University of Delaware
American University	George Washington University	Old Dominion University	University of Denver
Amherst College	Georgetown University	Penn State University	University of Florida
Arizona State University	Georgia Tech	Pepperdine University	University of Georgia
Auburn University	Gettysburg College	Pitzer College	University of Illinois
Babson College	Gonzaga University	Pomona College	University of Iowa
Ball State University	Goucher College	Princeton University	University of Kansas
Bard College	Grinnell College	Providence College	University of Kentucky
Barnard College	Grove City College	Purdue University	University of Maine
Bates College	Guilford College	Reed College	University of Maryland
Baylor University	Gustavus Adolphus College	Rensselaer Polytechnic Institute	University of Massachusetts
Beloit College	Hamilton College	Rhode Island School of Design	University of Miami
Bentley College	Hampshire College	Rhodes College	University of Michigan
Binghamton University	Hampton University	Rice University	University of Minnesota
Birmingham Southern College	Hanover College	Rochester Institute of Technology	University of Mississippi
Boston College	Harvard University	Rollins College	University of Missouri
Boston University	Harvey Mudd College	Rutgers University	University of Nebraska
Bowdoin College	Haverford College	San Diego State University	University of New Hampshire
Brandeis University	Hofstra University	Santa Clara University	University of North Carolina
Brigham Young University	Hollins University	Sarah Lawrence College	University of Notre Dame
Brown University	Howard University	Scripps College	University of Oklahoma
Bryn Mawr College	Idaho State University	Seattle University	University of Oregon
Bucknell University	Illinois State University	Seton Hall University	University of Pennsylvania
Cal Poly	Illinois Wesleyan University	Simmons College	University of Pittsburgh
Cal Poly Pomona	Indiana University	Skidmore College	University of Puget Sound
Cal State Northridge	Iowa State University	Slippery Rock	University of Rhode Island
Cal State Sacramento	Ithaca College	Smith College	University of Richmond
Caltech	IUPUI	Southern Methodist University	University of Rochester
Carleton College	James Madison University	Southwestern University	University of San Diego
Carnegie Mellon University	Johns Hopkins University	Spelman College	University of San Francisco
Case Western Reserve	Juniata College	St. Joseph's University Philladelphia	University of South Carolina
Centenary College of Louisiana	Kansas State	St. John's University	University of South Dakota
Centre College	Kent State University	St. Louis University	University of South Florida
Claremont McKenna College	Kenyon College	St. Olaf College	University of Southern California
Clark Atlanta University	Lafayette College	Stanford University	University of Tennessee
Clark University	LaRoche College	Stetson University	University of Texas
Clemson University	Lawrence University	Stony Brook University	University of Utah
Colby College	Lehigh University	Susquhanna University	University of Vermont
Colgate University	Lewis & Clark College	Swarthmore College	University of Virginia
College of Charleston	Louisiana State University	Syracuse University	University of Washington
College of the Holy Cross	Loyola College in Maryland	Temple University	University of Wisconsin
College of William & Mary	Loyola Marymount University	Tennessee State University	UNLV
College of Wooster	Loyola University Chicago	Texas A & M University	Ursinus College
Colorado College	Loyola University New Orleans	Texas Christian University	Valparaiso University
Columbia University	Macalester College	Towson University	Vanderbilt University
Connecticut College	Marlboro College	Trinity College Connecticut	Vassar College
Cornell University	Marquette University	Trinity University Texas	Villanova Unversity
Creighton University	McGill University	Truman State	Virginia Tech
CUNY Hunters College	Miami University of Ohio	Tufts University	Wake Forest University
Dartmouth College	Michigan State University	Tulane University	Warren Wilson College
Davidson College	Middle Tennessee State	UC Berkeley	Washington and Lee University
Denison University	Middlebury College	UC Davis	Washington University in St. Louis
DePauw University	Millsaps College	UC Irvine	Wellesley College
Dickinson College	MIT	UC Riverside	Wesleyan University
Drexel University	Montana State University	UC San Diego	West Point
Duke University	Mount Holyoke College	UC Santa Barbara	West Virginia University
Duquesne University	Muhlenberg College	UC Santa Cruz	Wheaton College IL
Earlham College	New York University	UCLA	Wheaton College MA
East Carolina University	North Carolina State	Union College	Whitman College
Elon University	Northeastern University	University at Albany	Wilkes University
Emerson College	Northern Arizona University	University at Buffalo	Williams College
Emory University	Northern Illinois University	University of Alabama	Xavier University
FIT	Northwestern University	University of Arizona	Yale University
Florida State University	Oberlin College	University of Central Florida	
Fordham University	Occidental College	University of Chicago	